# Plagve

### A Rod for Run-awayes.

## Gods Tokens,

Of his fearful Iudgements, sundry wayes pronounced
vpon this City, and on seuerall persons, both flying from it,
and staying in it.

*Expressed in many dreadfull Examples of sudden Death, falne vpon both young and
old, within this City, and the Suburbes, in the Fields, and open Streets, to the
terrour of all those who liue, and to the warning of those who are to
dye, to be ready when God Almighty shall bee pleased
to call them.*

*By* T h o. D.

Lord, haue mercy    on London.

I follow.    We fly.

Wee dye.

Keepeout

Printed at London for *Iohn Trundle*, and are to be sold at his Shop in Smithfield, 1625.

# DEATH, DISEASE AND FAMINE
### IN PRE-INDUSTRIAL ENGLAND

DATE DUE I

Leslie Clarkson

# DEATH, DISEASE AND FAMINE
In Pre-industrial England

Gill and Macmillan

First published in 1975

Gill and Macmillan Ltd
15/17 Eden Quay
Dublin 1
and internationally through
association with the
Macmillan Publishers Group

7171 0729 9

Printed and bound in England by
Bristol Typesetting Co. Ltd  Barton Manor  St Philips

# Contents

# List of Illustrations
## FRONT AND BACK ENDPAPERS
### FAMINE
Hans Holbein : 'The Death of a Young Child' from *The Dance of Death* (1547). Holbein's series of woodcuts shows death visiting all strata of society and all ages. In this illustration, death plucks the young child from the cottage of his sorrowing parents. The apparent plumpness of the victim contrasts uneasily with the poverty of the home and does not suggest, as was in fact the case, that child deaths often resulted from under-nourishment or from diseases made more dangerous by malnutrition.

### PLAGUE
Frontispiece to Thomas Dekker's *A Rod for Run-awayes* (1625). In addition to the *Wonderful Year* which describes the London plague of 1603, Dekker produced several other accounts of plague, including a description of the epidemic of 1625. The illustration suggests the affliction coming down from heaven. Fleeing Londoners are met in hostile fashion by country-dwellers, while some are already dying behind haystacks. The identical plate, except for the captions, was used in the plague year of 1636 by an enterprising publisher who re-issued John Taylor's *Fearful Summer* written, like the *Rod for Run-awayes*, to describe the epidemic of 1625.

### SURGERY
A sixteenth-century woodcut of a surgeon and his mate at the battle-field. Surgery developed in close association with armies. In the background the battle rages between pikemen and musketeers, supported by artillery. The surgeon removes a pike head—or possibly an arrow, although no bowmen can be seen—from a remarkably unperturbed patient.

### PHYSIC
A diagram of a 'blood-letting man', 1475. The connection between astrology and early medicine was close. The signs of the zodiac, for example, were said to determine what part of the body should be selected for blood-letting. Diagrams such as this were published to assist physicians in diagnosis and treatment.

# Preface

THE purpose of history, it has been said, is part entertainment and part edification. The ostensible aim of this book is the first of these, but I hope that in the process the second will also be achieved. It ranges fairly widely over some of the field of historical demography, a subject that has only recently emerged as an important part of social history. The book's approach is not exclusively academic, for, although historical demography is concerned specifically with ordinary human beings—our own ancestors—its findings have scarcely ever been presented in a form comprehensible to the layman.

If demography is 'the quantitative study of human populations', then historical demography is that study extended back into past periods. It is concerned with gathering statistical information about the growth and movements of population, and with measuring fertility, mortality, marriage, family size and structure, which are the mechanisms by which total populations rise or fall. The findings have relevance far beyond the area of demography, for demographic trends influence and are influenced by political, religious and social events of all kinds. For example, wars, by separating husbands from wives, by causing death and spreading disease, affect both fertility and mortality. A change in the laws of inheritance or a government decision to impose extra taxation might influence the average age at which marriages take place, thus causing variations in marital fertility. The examples could be multiplied. They all show clearly how historical demography is inseparable from general history and how it can be a vital aid in our understanding of the past.

Unfortunately historical demography is not an easy subject for laymen to tackle. For one thing, few countries, and certainly not England, possess national censuses of population before the nineteenth century. Any demographic study, therefore, which investigates any period before the recent past, must make use of incomplete data, most of which were not gathered for demographic purposes at all. Sometimes the potential usefulness of such evidence is not immediately obvious. For example, parish registers have been known to historians for many years, but it is only in the last decade or two that their value as a source of information about such recondite issues as age of marriages, age-specific fertility and mortality, birth intervals, pre-nuptial pregnancies and duration of marriages has been appreciated. Then there is the further problem of methodology. Historical demography being quantitative, its methods of presentation and analysis are statistical; the investigator—and the reader of the results—needs to be adequately versed in the language of mathematics. A further difficulty is that the collection of data is very laborious and its subsequent analysis so tedious that it requires the aid of a computer. For all the effort absorbed by historical demography, its output so far has been modest.

It would be a pity, however, if the exciting vistas opened by this relatively young branch of social history were restricted to professional historians: when historians are reduced to talking only to themselves, the study of history ceases to have any value to society at large. This book is an attempt to creep up on historical demography unawares, so to speak. It focuses on one of the major differences between the history of population in England during the nineteenth and twentieth centuries and its history in earlier periods: the high and fluctuating mortality characteristic of the years before 1800. It deals with such

questions as: Why was mortality so high? What did our ancestors die of? What were the connections between harvests and death? What contribution, if any, did medicine make in reducing mortality? What effects did high mortality have on survivors? I am not a historical demographer, and the discussions of these questions are intended for the 'general reader', whoever he (or she) may be. I am conscious that my answers are incomplete and superficial, but I hope they may stimulate readers to discover more for themselves. For that purpose, and to acknowledge those works I have found useful, a bibliography is included. Notes have been used only to identify the sources of quotations.

I am grateful to Dr K. D. Brown, a fellow non-demographer, for his comments on the manuscript and to Mary Dowey of Gill and Macmillan for encouraging—cajoling?—me into finishing. As always, my wife, whose experience of demography is more practical than mine, deserves credit at this customary point in the preface.

# I

# The Harvest of Death

At the turn of the eighteenth and nineteenth centuries England's economy and society was transformed by industrialisation. Before the mid-eighteenth century the pace of economic change and population growth had been very slow, and the England of the early 1700s would not have been entirely unfamiliar to an Englishman from the seventeenth or even the sixteenth century. But an eighteenth-century Englishman, pitchforked magically into the future, would hardly have recognised the highly complex world of the later twentieth century, a world based on science and technology and held together by an intricate web of economic interrelationships. One feature might have impressed itself on his bewildered mind although not in a precise way: for every person living in England in the 1760s or 1770s there were seven or eight in the 1960s or 1970s. There have been few more dramatic changes over the last two centuries than the great growth of population experienced, not only in Britain and Europe, but throughout the whole world. This increase has come about not so much because of a rise in the birth rate—indeed fertility has fallen sharply in most western countries in the last century or so—but through a reduction in mortality. Before the Industrial Revolution England experienced high death rates that largely cancelled out the prolific fertility of the age. These high levels of mortality were among the most characteristic features of pre-industrial England and contrast sharply with the experience of the nineteenth and twentieth centuries.

In England today eleven or twelve people per thousand of the population die annually, a rate that varies little from year to year. There are no firm figures for mortality before 1837, when the civil registration of deaths commenced, but parish registers kept by Anglican churches from 1538 offer some clues to fluctuations in mortality in earlier centuries. At the end of the seventeenth century the 'normal' death rate in England—that is, the death rate in years which produced reasonable harvests and which were free from major epidemic—was about thirty per thousand, roughly two and a half times greater than the present level. But whereas today the death rate is fairly constant, in pre-industrial England it was highly volatile. When the harvests failed or epidemics struck, annual mortality doubled, trebled, or even, in particular localities, rose ten or twelve times higher than normal levels. Subsequently, as harvests improved and epidemics receded, the levels of mortality fell, perhaps to below normal for a while, as the population, culled of its more sickly members, enjoyed a restored supply of food and respite from disease.

Death in pre-industrial England, therefore, was a constant companion, as natural as eating and sleeping, as commonplace as birth, and practically as frequent. The pre-industrial birthrate was also high, generally in the mid-thirties per thousand, rising to forty or more when the age structure of the population was favourable. These levels were more than twice today's birth rate: in the marriage bed at least pre-industrial Englishmen and their wives outstripped the productivity of their twentieth-century counterparts. Yet their efforts did not result in a rapidly increasing population, for although there was usually a bigger traffic to the font than to the graveyard, fertility fluctuated much less from year to year than deaths, with the result that the surplus of births accumulated in a few years was frequently wiped out by a single year of unusually high mortality. Population increase before the Industrial Revolution, therefore, was only part of a continual ebbing and flowing of a tide which advanced to new high levels, only to run back again suddenly.

In the twentieth century world population grows rapidly and babies are regarded as pollution, threatening to upset the ecological balance by swamping the supply of space available for each individual. It needs an effort of imagination to realise that before the nineteenth century Europeans inhabited a world of empty acres which they only slowly peopled. In the 1340s England and Wales contained at least 3·7 million people, but the Black Death that ravaged the country between 1348 and 1350 reduced the population by a quarter or a third. The population continued to fall thereafter until at least the middle of the fifteenth century. It showed little sign of increasing before 1500, when it was probably not much more than 2·5 million. During the next 150 years, however, it roughly doubled, a small enough increase compared to the 36 million added in the century and a half after 1801, but causing, nevertheless, severe strains on available food resources. By the 1640s the population of England and Wales was between 5 million and 5·5 million, but it then stagnated once more. In 1700 it was still below 6 million and by 1750 was barely 6·3 million. But by then the country and the whole of western Europe was on the verge of a population explosion in which numbers multiplied more rapidly and more *consistently* than at any time in previous history.

The slow rate of population growth before 1750 was one consequence of the high and erratic mortality of the period; another was the short life-span of pre-industrial Englishmen. According to the Bible, three score years and ten was the appointed limit of human life, but statistical precision and divine truths do not always coincide. In the 1970s the average Englishman can, at birth, expect to last for sixty-eight years; women actually exceed their biblical allowance by four years. In the mid-nineteenth century life expectancies were forty-one for men and forty-five for women, probably much the same as in the eighteenth century. But seventeenth-century Englishmen could not expect to survive beyond their mid-thirties, although their Elizabethan forebears seem to have been able to hold on to about forty. These chronological variations are a matter to which we shall return.

Short average life expectancies do not, of course, mean an absence of old people. A child surviving to manhood in the seventeenth century had a one in four chance of reaching seventy and a one in sixteen chance of achieving eighty. Nevertheless, the average age of dying for adults was in the fifties and the elderly were in short supply. Old age was, in consequence, the occasion of veneration, curiosity, and sometimes hostility. 'Age, I do abhor thee, Youth, I do adore thee,' wrote Shakespeare. The educated displayed towards old people in the sixteenth and seventeenth centuries something of the attitudes displayed towards old buildings in the twentieth: they were objects to be investigated, recorded and conserved. At death the ages of the elderly were inscribed in parish registers (which, in the normal course of things, rarely bothered with such information) and chiselled on tombstones for the information of posterity. Individual old men and women were occasionally plucked from their parishes by the well-to-do and put on public display. The most celebrated old man in seventeenth-century England was Thomas Parr of Winnington in Shropshire, turned into a sideshow in 1635 by the Earl of Arundel, the theme of a poem, 'The Old, Old, Very Old Man', by John Taylor the 'Water Poet', and the subject of an autopsy following his death at the age of 152 (or so it was said) performed by William Harvey, the famous physician. Parr had led an anonymous and uneventful life until he married for the first time when he was eighty. Twenty-five years later his affections were caught wandering, and he was compelled to stand in church clad in a white sheet as a penance for adultery. A second marriage followed at 112, to the stated satisfaction of his new wife. The Earl of Arundel brought Parr to London as a curiosity forty years later, where he promptly succumbed to the 'smoke of sulpherous coal constantly used as fuel for fires' and the more 'generous rich and varied diet, and stronger drink'[1] than had been available in Shropshire. He was interred in Westminster Abbey, while Harvey wrote up his autopsy with a clinical care that contrasted strangely with his credulous acceptance of Parr's reputed age. Some years later another medical man, John Locke, took an interest in an old woman, Alice George, who claimed to be 108 in 1680. Neither Parr nor Alice could match the longevity of Henry Jenkin, a vigorous 169-year-old who died in 1670.

Death harvested the young much more abundantly than the old, and, in contrast to extreme age, infant mortality passed almost without comment. When virtually every family experienced at least one dead child, an infant corpse had little novelty, although a resigned parent, wishing his Christian name to be passed on to his descendants, might give it to all his baby sons by way of insurance against the ceaseless convoy from cot to coffin. Just how prevalent infant mortality was is difficult to determine with precision. Modern British experience suggests a figure of twenty per thousand (i.e. twenty infants dying within their first twelve months for every thousand live births during the year), compared with 140–150 per thousand a century ago. Pre-industrial levels were higher: they were possibly in the general region of 150–200 per thousand, and considerably greater in overcrowded urban communities and during the sickly years of epidemics or food shortages.

But the vagueness of the statistical evidence cannot hide the brutal reality that entry into this world and the first months of existence were the most dangerous period of human life. Childbirth frequently occurred in dirty, overcrowded conditions, attended by untutored midwives whose obstetric skills had been refined by groping and fumbling, and assisted by assorted neighbours who busied themselves by casting horoscopes, muttering incantations, shutting doors, blocking windows, and spreading infection. If the baby survived, against all the odds, the mother often did not, leaving the infant to manage the best it could with a foster-mother. Foster or natural, mothers were often ill-nourished and burdened with heavy physical toil around house and farm, and their infants ill-prepared to resist the childish ailments which are so trivial today but which were so calamitous then. Possibly upper-class infants had a better chance of survival than those of the poor, although the evidence does not suggest any major class differences in the rates of infant mortality. The wealthy had the doubtful benefit of physicians, and during the sixteenth and seventeenth centuries obstetrical knowledge was improved by Paré, Vesalius and the Chamberlens. But their practices were applied largely by others, for example by midwives instructed from such books as *The Garden of Roses for Pregnant Women and Midwives*, published in Germany in 1513 and reissued in 1555 under the title *The Birth of Mankind*. As is often the case with textbooks, they fell into the hands of those less skilled than the authors, a fact recognised in 1682 by the publisher of *The Complete English Midwife*, which was designed to be 'fitted for the meanest capacities' of reader.

In one respect the children of the upper classes lived a more hazardous life than those socially less favoured: the widespread practice among the wealthy of wet-nursing was a fashion adopted for the convenience of the mother rather than the health of the child. The risks of wet-nursing were implied in the advice given regarding the selection of a nurse. According to one fifteenth-century manual, she should be 'not too young and not too old. She must at all times be free from illness of the eyes or body. . . . Mark also, that she must be neither too slim, nor too plump. . . . She must have a good character, modest, chaste and clean.'[2] Despite attention to such details, mishaps could occur if, for example, the nurse over-indulged in a diet of onions or highly salted food, which tainted her milk, or engaged in strenuous exercise which caused her to run dry. Then the remedy recommended was a régime of peas, beans and gruel. An accident to the nurse threatened the whole management of the child. In May 1727 Mrs Townsend, foster-mother to the infant son of the third Earl of Cardigan, 'fell down in the stone court, it being wet and slippery, and broke both the bones of her arm about three inches above her right hand'. The Earl was away from home, but his faithful steward, who attended to nursery matters as assiduously as he collected his master's outstanding rents, gelded horses and sold timber from the estate,

> immediately sent for Mr Fryer who came and set it before eight. We do not suffer Master Robert to suck for these five or six days, for these things are always attended with a feaver. My mother and Mrs Bradshaw will take care of the child, and the nurse's sister is with her.

Three days later another letter was sent to the Earl:

> Master James [an elder son] and Master Robert are very well; and the nurse is entirely free from pain, and has not been feavourish as we could perceive, so that in a day or two the child may suck without any manner of danger. Her breasts have been very regularly drawn all this time, and Master Robert has born the loss of the pap with a great deal of patience.[3]

The seven-month-old Robert was not only patient but unusually adaptable, for it was common practice not to wean babies until well after their first birthday. However, he was reunited with Mrs Townsend within another three days, although reports on her condition continued to be sent to the father until the end of the month. During the correspondence there was no mention of the Countess, whose part in her son's rearing seems to have ended as soon as labour was completed.

If the threats to life were greatest in the first twelve months, they did not retreat very far during the remainder of childhood. Child death rates (i.e. for the ages of one to fourteen years) were always above one hundred per thousand, and they often rose above two hundred. Added to the death rates for infants (i.e. babies aged less than twelve months), these figures mean that in pre-industrial England between thirty and forty per cent of babies born alive never survived to fifteen years of age. Girls were a little more hard-wearing than boys; then, as now, mortality among males of all ages was higher than for females. Even so, roughly one-third of all baby girls never lived long enough to become mothers themselves. In this way infant and child mortality had a cumulatively depressing effect on the growth of population. In the same way, too, the number of children in a normal pre-industrial household was kept down to between two and three; the image of families of teeming children is largely the product of the nineteenth century, an age which found ways of reducing the loss of infant lives more readily than ways of cutting the number of conceptions.

Pre-industrial England was not uniformly unhealthy. Not only did mortality vary from year to year, but some places and regions were decidedly more deadly than others. On the uplands of the north and west the winters were wet and cold and the summers wet and cool; the crops grew thinly and margins of subsistence were narrow. Here, more than in the more fertile districts, a poor harvest brought dearth and famine. In lowland England there were extensive undrained marshes bordering coasts and rivers, which harboured fevers and agues harmful to children and adults alike. Daniel Defoe visited the marshy district of Essex in 1722 and was inform'd that . . . there was a farmer, who was then living with the five and twentieth wife, and that his son who was but about thirty-five years old, had already had about fourteen. . . . The reason, as a merry fellow told me, who said he had had about a dozen and half of wives (tho' I found afterwards he fibb'd a little) was this; That they being bred in the marshes themselves, and season'd to the place, did pretty well with it; but that they always went up into the hilly country . . . for a wife: That when they took the young lasses out of the wholesome and fresh air, they were healthy, fresh and clear, and well; but when they came out of their native air into the marshes among the fogs and damps, there they presently changed their complexion, got an ague or two, and seldom held it above half a year, or a year at most; and then, said he, we go to the uplands again, and fetch another. . . . It is true, the fellow told this in a kind of drollery and mirth; but the fact, for all that, is certainly true; and that they have abundance of wives by that very means: Nor is it less true, that the inhabitants in these places do not hold it out, as in other countries. . . .[4]

The unhealthiest places were the towns, where everything worked in favour of high mortality. Poor people lived in congested houses and were particularly susceptible to epidemics: bubonic plague, for example, was overwhelmingly a disease of the city. Towns were dirty, water supplies were tainted, and sewerage was disposed of inadequately or not at all. True, towns had a near monopoly of doctors and hospitals as well as a disproportionate amount of sickness, but medicine was primarily the handmaiden of death. In one way urban dwellers were especially vulnerable. Most of them worked in commerce or manufacturing and depended on the market for their food and fuel; they therefore felt the full force of rising prices in times of shortage, unprotected by rights of commonage or the possession of a garden plot. By the sixteenth century many of the larger towns kept stocks of corn which the authorities sold to the poor, sometimes below market prices, in an attempt to stave off starvation. Paradoxically, however, these sometimes made things worse, since paupers were attracted from the rural districts in the hope of getting food. Towns were always venues for vagrants searching for casual employment; they arrived weak and wretched and gravitated to the poorest and most overcrowded districts, where they were readily recruited to the ranks of the diseased.

The largest and most lethal city was London. Its growth was one of the most remarkable social phenomena in early modern England. At the beginning of the sixteenth century it contained between 50,000 and 60,000 people, or some two or three per cent of the total population of the country. Two centuries later over 500,000 people, that is ten per cent of the entire population of England and Wales, lived in the metropolis. In London the death rate exceeded the birth rate even in normal years of the seventeenth and eighteenth centuries, for the crowded conditions of living in the capital made it an ideal breeding-ground for epidemics of all kind. In the plague year of 1603, 43,000 people died—not all of plague; in 1625, 63,000; and in 1665, 97,000. In such bad years up to one-quarter of London's inhabitants finished in the city's graveyards. Even in normal years of the late seventeenth and early eighteenth centuries, annual deaths in the metropolis totalled roughly between 20,000 and 28,000, implying a death rate of forty or fifty per thousand. London continued to expand only because of its ability to attract migrants from the surrounding countryside. During the second half of the seventeenth century an average of 8,000 newcomers arrived in the metropolis each year. Some were gentlemen, come to spend the season in London or to taste the pleasures of court life; such people quickly retreated in the face of epidemic disease. Others were landowners involved in lengthy litigation in Chancery, which not infrequently petered out with the death of one of the parties. Many came as apprentices to city merchants and tradesmen or to study at the Inns of Court; and many more drifted to the metropolis in search of a job and a room to rent and found instead an unmarked grave.

As we have seen, death rates in pre-industrial England fluctuated from year to year and place to place. There were also long-term shifts in levels of mortality. The Black Death of 1348–50 seems to have marked the onset of one such shift. The initial loss of a large part of the English population was followed by more than a century of further decline and stagnation. Historians are still arguing about the causes of this extended demographic depression. It may have been caused by reduction in fertility brought about by women marrying in, say, their late twenties instead of their early twenties: such a postponement would reduce the number of child-bearing years within marriage. But there is no firm evidence that this happened, and it does not seem very probable, since after the Black Death there was plenty of land available at low rents, so that people would presumably have been able to marry sooner rather than later. It seems more likely that the check to population growth in the late fourteenth and fifteenth centuries was caused by a generally higher level of mortality, though for what reasons we do not know. Bubonic plague, it has been suggested, acted like the steady drizzle of rain upon a leaking roof. The deluge of the Black Death opened up cracks in the ceiling and plague continued to drip into the community below even after the first downpour had abated. However, plague flourished best in overcrowded urban conditions, and although it returned several times in the late fourteenth and fifteenth centuries, it does not seem to have been virulent enough to cause a continuous reduction of the population. It was probably assisted in its lethal activities by other diseases such as fevers of various kinds, typhus, dysentery, and diarrhoea, turning the period into 'the golden age of bacteria',[5] not only in England but throughout the whole of western Europe.

Was the sixteenth century any healthier? The expectation of life may have become longer than it had been in the fifteenth century, and higher than it was to be during the seventeenth century: the average age at death appears to have been in the forties rather than the thirties. Certainly, from about 1500 the population of England and Europe started to grow with a vigour unknown during the previous 150 years. Increasing fertility had something to do with this increase. In Worcester, for example, the age of first marriage of women fell during the first three-quarters of the sixteenth century, and the number of children born to marriages therefore increased. A similar pattern of events probably occurred elsewhere. But rising fertility was only one part of the equation: there was also a general fall in mortality, although for what reasons are not clear. Food supplies became scarcer as the population increased, and the poor became less well fed and thus more vulnerable to illness. On the other hand, the golden age of bacteria turned a little tarnished. Plague at least was absent in major epidemic form until 1563, and some other maladies may have become less prevalent than they had been in the fifteenth century or were to become again in the seventeenth. This is not to say that the sixteenth century was free from periods of heavy mortality. Disease was still rife, and in the late 1550s there was a mortality crisis of serious proportions throughout much of England caused by a severe epidemic of influenza and other fevers. For about five years death rates were well above normal until the crisis passed. The population grew again, although new peaks could hardly have been reached until the 1570s. There was excessively high mortality again in 1587–88, but it receded; and early in the next decade a contemporary was able to exclaim that 'We have not, God be thanked, been touched with any extreme mortality, either by sword or sickness, that might abate the over-grown number of us.'[6]

He spoke too soon. The year 1593 was marked by a recurrence of fatal disease, and 1596–98 were desperately dangerous years during which high mortality occurred in many parts of the country. Burials were two, three and even four times higher than normal; during the great plague in Penrith in 1598 burials were almost thirteen times greater than in normal years. Over the whole country the population fell as mortality exceeded fertility. However, in the early seventeenth century population resumed its increase for a time until, in the second quarter of the century, the death rate shifted to a higher plane than it had occupied during the previous century and a quarter. In the little Devonshire village of Colyton the new era was ushered in dramatically by an outbreak of plague in 1646 during which almost one-fifth of the entire village was buried. When the disease abated, mortality rates in Colyton did not fall to their previous levels but remained relatively high for the next eighty years. This experience seems to have been repeated in many other places, although the reasons for it are as mysterious as the turnabout in long-term trends that took place earlier. Possibly the growth of population up to the 1620s had so stretched food supplies that the population was less well nourished and therefore more susceptible to disease. Perhaps the bacteria were establishing a second golden age. Furthermore, not only did mortality rise, but so did the age of first marriage, with the result that marital fertility declined. With increased mortality and reduced fertility, population rose very slowly in England during the last three-quarters of the seventeenth century, although by the end of the century there were signs that the population was growing vigorously once more in the Home Counties, the Midlands and parts of the north-west.

This renewed growth was checked in the late 1690s and again in 1708–10, which were particularly unhealthy years. During the 1720s and early 1730s the death rate throughout England as a whole rose above the birth rate. For two decades the population of the country fell, and it was only from the 1740s that a substantial gap again opened up between births and deaths. This time it did not close. England was on the eve of a vital revolution with peaks of high mortality occurring less regularly and the general death rate falling. By the end of the eighteenth century 'there were not only more births but also more survivals in each year'.[7] An era in the history of mortality was ending; a new era of sustained population growth was just beginning.

Why did our ancestors die in such profusion before the Industrial Revolution? There were three main interlocking reasons. The first was the poor environment in which they lived. The most important element here was the inadequate food supply. The diet of the masses was unbalanced and frequently insufficient; in years of poor harvests food was scarce, and occasionally there was starvation. Hence the population was vulnerable to deficiency diseases and easy prey to all kinds of illness. Secondly, there were epidemics which killed in large numbers. Some, like plague, malaria and typhus, have long since disappeared from England, although they are still found in underdeveloped parts of the world. Others such as smallpox were endemic, but flared into epidemic proportions from time to time and ravaged the population practically unchecked. Thirdly, the nature of diseases was not understood and the manner of their transmission was a mystery. Physicians were powerless to deal with ailments that would be minor today, and they were unable to stem the tide of death that ran so swiftly over the population. There were other causes of death too—war, accidents and violence—but their contributions to mortality were minor compared with the ravages of dearth and disease.

# 2

# The Fear of Famine

THE connection between food supplies and the growth of population has long been appreciated. It was the basis of the famous *Essay on Population* by the Rev. T. R. Malthus, first published in 1798, in which he argued that there was a natural tendency for population to grow faster than the supply of food, with the result that any increase in numbers would be checked by famine, pestilence and war. If, as a result of a run of good harvests, the supply of food increased, the poor would marry younger and produce more babies, creating shortage of food once more and so eventually bringing the increase to a halt. Malthus wrote at the end of a century during which the population of England and Wales increased from just under six million to just over nine million without any discernible fall in standards of nutrition. He wrote also on the eve of a century during which there occurred unprecedented increases in population. Malthus did not allow for advances in agricultural productivity that were already taking place when he published his essay, nor for improvements in economic organisation that made possible a tremendous development of trade in agricultural products. In fact there is no firm evidence that fertility ever increased because the supply of food increased, nor that famine was a recurring accompaniment of human existence in England. It is by no means certain that pre-industrial England ever experienced the full horrors of a Malthusian subsistence crisis.

Nevertheless, until the very end of the eighteenth century there were risks of serious harvest failures which could not be made good by importing supplies from over-seas. Shortfalls in the harvest caused food prices to rise and provoked great hardship among the poor. Further-more, any sustained increase in population faster than the growth of agricultural productivity had much the same effect. As Alderman Box of London told the government in 1576, at a time when the population of England was rising, 'The people are increassid and grounde for plowes dothe wante, Corn and all other victuall is scante, many strangers sufferid heare, which make the corne and vic-tuall deare.'[1] In the short run, therefore, a sequence of bad harvests might well push up the death rate, rarely, perhaps, directly as the result of starvation, but more usually through belt-tightening and malnutrition, which made people more susceptible to a host of illnesses. Pre-industrial Englishmen lived in the ever-present fear of going hungry.

Before the Industrial Revolution the population of England lived chiefly on a diet of cereals. The grain most widely grown and consumed was barley. It thrived in a variety of soils and climates, and could be baked into loaves, brewed into beer, or distilled into gin. Rye, either alone or mixed with barley or wheat, was generally eaten in the north of the country. Oats, as Dr Johnson remarked, was a grain 'which in England is generally given to horses, but in Scotland supports the people'.[2] Contrary to popular belief, wheaten bread did not con-stitute the staple diet of the majority of Englishmen before the eighteenth century. Because of its high price wheat was an important cash crop for farmers, but compared with the other grains it was fickle in its requirements as to soil and climate. Hence the acreage grown was com-paratively small until in the late seventeenth century, when falling grain prices encouraged farmers to concen-trate on wheat as the crop that commanded the highest price in the market. Corn diets were supplemented by fruit and vegetables (including potatoes after the early eighteenth century), milk, butter, and cheese. In the country, meat was a fairly common component of the diets of farmers and those farm labourers who lived with their employers. Other rural dwellers ate meat, provided they enjoyed rights of commonage or possessed a small garden plot on which to keep a cow, pig or poultry. Completely landless labourers were less fortunate, for they had to buy their food in the market, apart from the occasional rabbit, hare, or game bird that they might be able to get by hunting or poaching. Urban dwellers were forced to rely completely on purchases in the market; and for the poor, once the essential bread and beer had been bought, there was very little money left for meat. Ale or beer was a necessary part of all diets in the absence of clean drinking water or tea and coffee which were not widely available before the eighteenth century. Fish was available in towns near the coast, but elsewhere it was scarce, expensive, and of poor quality.

A diet composed of grain, meat, dairy products, fruit, and vegetables is admirable provided it is available in sufficient quantity and the right balance. But there were great social variations in the style in which people ate. In the mid-sixteenth century the English aristocracy were renowned for the style of their housekeeping, maintaining 'very grand establishments, both with regard to the great abundance of eatables consumed by them as also by reason of the numerous attendants, in which they exceed all other nations'.[3] One aristocratic household at the beginning of the seventeenth century consumed in a single week twenty-three sheep and lambs, two bullocks, one veal, fifty-nine chickens, capons and pullets, five pigs, twenty-four pigeons, and fifty-four rabbits. Aristocratic households spent great sums on food, even though 'a great housekeeper is sure of nothing for his good cheare save a great Turd at his gate'. Lower down the social scale, the county gentry entertained on a scale only a little less lavish than the nobility. Before the Civil War Sir Hugh Chomley, a Yorkshire gentleman, regularly dispensed hospitality on a large scale, as is apparent from his own account:

> I had between thirty and forty in my ordinary family, a chaplain who said prayers every morning at six, and again before dinner and supper, a porter who merely attended the gates, which were ever shut before dinner, when the bell was rung to prayers, and not opened till one o'clock, except for strangers who came to dinner, which was ever fit to receive three or four besides my family, without any trouble; whatever their fare was they were sure to have a hearty welcome. Twice a week a certain number of old people, widows and indigent persons, were served at my gates with bread and good pottage made of beef, which I mention that those that succeed may follow the example.[4]

Further still down the social pyramid, sturdy yeomen farmers prided themselves on their hospitality, entertaining guests on 'bread, beer and Beof, yeoman's fare; we have no kickshaws: full dishes, whole bellyfuls'.[5]

Statements of this kind have sometimes been taken to suggest that there existed a well-fed 'merrie England' before the Industrial Revolution. On the contrary, they are evidence of the concentration of resources into a very few hands, and of restricted markets offering the wealthy only a very limited range of consumption goods. Looking back at instances of lavish hospitality in the sixteenth and seventeenth centuries, Adam Smith, writing in *The Wealth of Nations* in 1776, commented that 'it seems to be common in all nations to whom commerce and manufacturers are little known'. In such economies 'a great proprietor, having nothing for which he can exchange the greater part of his produce of his lands which is over and above the maintenance of the cultivators, consumes the whole in rustic hospitality at home'.[6] For the wealthy, eating was a form of social ostentation at a time when there was little else to spend money on, and, for the country gentry, entertainment was a relief from the intolerable tedium of rural life, rather in the way that meal-times are today eagerly awaited on long ocean voyages. Among poor people, periodic feastings at Christmas, harvest times, weddings, baptisms and funerals were a respite from the monotonous and stinted diets of everyday life.

The decline of hospitality, and the consequential impoverishment of those who depended on it, was a recurring complaint from the sixteenth to the eighteenth centuries. In 1587 William Harrison lamented the 'decaie of house-keeping whereby the poor have been relieved'.[7] In 1632 the government issued a proclamation forbidding the country gentry from taking up residence in London. By coming to the capital, it was alleged, the income from their estates in the countryside was spent in London instead of 'whence it ariseth, nor are the people of them relieved therewith, or by their hospitality, nor yet set on work, as they might be and would be'.[8] In the following century Adam Smith noted that his prosperous age no longer maintained the standards of hospitality of former times.

However sumptuous the scale of housekeeping practised by the great landowners, it had only a tiny influence on the patterns of consumption of the bulk of the population. Among the poorer sections of society something like four-fifths of income was spent on food, compared with one-fifth or one-quarter today. The bulk of expenditure went on grain, and the state of the harvest therefore determined whether people ate well or badly. If corn was cheap, people had money to spend on meat, dairy products, fruit and vegetables; when corn was dear, bread and beer consumed every penny. Nor was that all. When the harvest was good there was cheap feed for cattle, straw for the winter, gleanings 'in the field from the cartes on the wayes, and aboute their howses, which dothe feede, nourrishe, and brede their hogges, geese, cockes, hennes, Duckes, Chyckins, and other poultry, which increaseth egges, mylke, butter, cheese, and other victual for the countery to live by'.[9]

Taking the long view, food supplies increased during the sixteenth, seventeenth and eighteenth centuries, enabling the population to grow and, by the end of the period, to raise its standards of consumption. Output was expanded by bringing more land into cultivation and by improving the productivity of land and labour through the adoption of better techniques and organisation. The one element beyond human control was the weather, which was as fickle in pre-industrial England as it is now. A predominantly agrarian economy with relatively simple farming techniques was particularly susceptible to the vagaries of wind and rain: years of bad weather were usually years of high food prices, and often, too, years of high mortality.

There is an enduring myth that English agriculture lacked a rational basis before the mid-eighteenth century and that farmers were unthinking conservatives wedded to old ways. In fact farming practices were adapted to local conditions of soil, climate and markets, and, within the limitations of existing knowledge, were capable of considerable modification. Tudor and Stuart Englishmen sometimes claimed with patriotic fervour that they were God's chosen people dwelling in a latter-day Garden of Eden. What God had in fact chosen to give them was a climate suitable for temperate agriculture and a fairly fertile country suited to plough and pasture, which, by the application of capital, labour and ingenuity, could be made to yield food and raw materials in sufficiency, if not in abundance. The basic pattern of agriculture was set by topography and temperature. The cool, damp uplands of the west and north were used mainly for the pasturing of stock. Large flocks of sheep were kept on the hills throughout summer and winter, producing sweet mutton and coarse wool for carpets and tweeds. Store cattle were raised for sale to the graziers of the Midlands and Home Counties, who fattened them for the urban meat markets. Corn was grown in the valleys and on the coastal plains for local consumption and for feeding to animals.

Further south and east, the lowland zone of England was given over to the production of corn and grass and supported many combinations of mixed farming. Sheep were kept on the chalklands, not so much for their wool or meat as for their manure. By day the flocks were grazed on the hillside pastures, and by night they were penned on the light soils of the arable fields where they dropped their dung, thus making the ground fertile for the production of barley and other grains. On heavier soils, cereals, peas and beans, cattle and sheep, were produced in various combinations. Generally the emphasis of farming was on the growing of corn for the market, but in all districts animals were kept for their dung and for haulage. They were grazed on meadows and commons, and also on arable fields after the harvest had been gathered in and during the fallow year. The fallow was necessary in practically all farming systems so that the ground could recover its fertility.

In some parts of lowland England, where the grass grew particularly lush, farmers specialised in meat production or dairying. Defoe reported from the Essex marshes in 1722 that 'Their chief business is breeding of calves, which I need not say are the best and fattest, and the largest veal in England, if not in the world.'[10] Essex farmers also bought sheep from graziers in Leicestershire and Lincolnshire during September and October, which they fattened up as 'marsh-mutton' for the Christmas market. In many areas of the Midlands the clay soils were heavy, good for grain but expensive to plough and drain; they were also good for cattle and sheep. The way the land was used in such regions was determined by the long-run relative price

B

trends of grain and pastoral products; generally speaking, as the seventeenth century progressed, farmers on the heavier soils tended to concentrate more and more on animals and animal products.

Food production was an enterprise carried out by landowners, tenant farmers and labourers. Together these groups comprised roughly two-thirds or more of the population, although the proportion declined gradually as the industrial and commercial sectors of the economy slowly grew in importance. The bulk of the land was cultivated by tenant farmers. Very many of them were copyholders, occupying their farms on tenures that passed from generation to generation, and paying rents and fines that could not be easily varied by their landlords. There was, however, an increasing number of leasehold tenures granted for a term of years, the rent of which could be readily adjusted to changing price levels; these forms of tenancies were obviously attractive to landlords in periods of rising prices. Landowners were essentially collectors of rents. They did not generally engage directly in farming themselves, except for the diminishing class of owner-occupiers. But they influenced farming practices in various ways: by the level of rents they were able to exact; by the covenants written into their leases regulating crop rotations, the numbers of animals to be kept, the use of timber and mineral rights and similar matters; and by the care or laxity with which they or their stewards presided at the manorial courts. In the early eighteenth century roughly one-quarter of England was still farmed on the common-field system; the proportion had probably been nearer to one-half two centuries earlier. In the common fields the farms were arranged, not in consolidated blocks, but as strips of land scattered throughout the arable fields, the strips of one farm being intermingled with those of another. Tenants also enjoyed the use of meadows and commons for the grazing of animals or the production of hay according to their rights in the arable

fields. This kind of farming required a degree of co-operation among cultivators, and it was the function of the
manorial court to organise crop rotations, control the
stocking of commons, determine field boundaries, super-
vise conditions of tenures, and attend to the myriad other
details of communal farming.

Many farmers worked their land with their own labour
and the labour of their families, but wage-labour became
increasingly common during the sixteenth, seventeenth
and eighteenth centuries. In the early sixteenth century
possibly one-quarter of the rural population worked for
wages as farm labourers either full-time or part-time,
although many of them also possessed small plots of land
of their own on which they worked as well. As the population increased so did the number of people without land.
By the mid-seventeenth century as much as half the rural
population were agricultural labourers for at least part
of the time. Some worked as day labourers; others were
hired by the year and lived in with the farmer and his
family, a system that remained common until the closing
years of the eighteenth century.

With the growth of population in pre-industrial England there was a need to increase food supplies. The key
to expanding production was to enlarge the quantity of
forage and fodder available to animals. Sheep and cattle
dung were the only really important sources of fertiliser:
so the more animals that could be kept, the greater
became the supply of dung for maintaining the fertility
of the existing cultivated land and for improving the fertility of soils not yet in regular cultivation because their
productivity was not high enough. Thus greater supplies
of fodder and forage supported more animals and thereby
indirectly helped to produce more grain, fruit, and vegetables, as well as more meat, butter, cheese, and milk.

During the sixteenth, seventeenth and eighteenth centuries English landlords and farmers made a concerted
attack on marsh, fen, forest, and heath, in an attempt to

bring more land into cultivation. At the turn of the six-teenth and seventeenth centuries large tracts of the East Anglian fens were drained, and drowned lands in other parts of the country were also reclaimed. Drainage and the subsequent work required to make the reclaimed land bear crops and support livestock was expensive, and it was therefore carried out by wealthy landowners during periods of rising farm prices and profits. Some landowners also created water-meadows in an effort to increase the supply of grass, though, like reclamation, they were expen-sive and the work could be undertaken only when profits were rising. On low-lying land alongside rivers flowing down from chalky hills, channels were dug to carry the water over the meadows in early winter. They remained flooded until late February, when the water was run off. This practice encouraged an early growth of grass that bridged the hungry gap between the diminishing stocks of winter fodder and new supplies of spring grass. Sub-sequent flooding in spring prepared the land for a couple of hay crops and summer grazing for cattle.

Another costly technique leading to increased pro-duction involved reorganising the scattered strips of the common fields into compact farms which were then used for convertible husbandry. Part of the farm, probably the biggest part, was kept as pasture for several years, during which time the animals dropped their dung and urine; the remainder was kept under a succession of crops. Then land-use was switched. The arable was allowed to revert to pasture, while part of the fertilised pasture was con-verted to tillage. A good deal of the Midland plain was being farmed in this manner by 1700. As a result the til-lage land yielded up to double the crop of permanent tillage land, and there was also an increased output of pastoral products. Convertible husbandry was also used on reclaimed marsh and fen and newly cleared forest and heathland.

From the middle of the seventeenth century root crops

such as carrots, swedes and turnips, legumes such as peas and beans, and improved grasses and clover, were introduced extensively into English field systems. They had been used to a limited extent even before 1600, but they were now used as field crops on the light chalky soils of the south and east, where they replaced the fallow. The benefits were twofold. By their ability to impart nitrogen the legumes contributed directly to the fertility of the soil; and, as a result of the increased supplies of animal feed that they provided, livestock populations were enlarged and more manure became available to use on the arable fields. As the fertility of the light soils rose they became the main areas of grain production in England, since they were relatively cheap to plough and drain and they were near to the main centres of population. The heavy clays of the Midlands, by contrast, came to specialise in livestock farming. At the beginning of the eighteenth century Defoe observed that Leicestershire, which a century before had been a mixed farming county with an emphasis on grain, 'seems to be taken up in country business . . . particularly in breeding and feeding cattle; the largest sheep and horses are found here, and hence it comes to pass too, that they are in consequence a vast magazine of wool for the rest of the nation'.[11] Root crops were less well suited to the heavy clay soils, and in those areas the fallow year survived as a feature of English farming until the nineteenth century.

English agriculture, then, was capable of increasing the output of corn, meat, dairy, vegetables, fruit, tobacco—the last-named until literally stamped out by Cromwell's troops in order to protect the monopoly of the Virginia Company—as well as industrial products such as hides, tallow, wool and dyestuffs. The problem is to know whether production was responsive enough to match the increase in population. It was not simply that there were two stomachs to be filled in the early eighteenth century for every one that had existed in 1500, but that a greater proportion of the population in the 1700s lived in towns and were employed in industry and commerce than had been the case earlier. There was therefore a greater dependent population to be fed by that proportion of the work-force still employed in agriculture. The very fact that urban, industrial and commercial life had developed in the sixteenth, seventeenth and eighteenth centuries suggests that considerable advances in agricultural productivity had taken place. Yet there had also been formidable obstacles to progress. Enterprise and innovation could be found among individuals at all levels, yet on the whole society viewed change with caution. 'It were good . . . that Men in their Innovations, would follow the Example of Time itselfe; what indeed Innovateth greatly, but quietly, and by degree, scarce to be perceived,' counselled Francis Bacon.[12] As John Aubrey reported in the later seventeenth century, 'Even to attempt an improvement in husbandry (though it succeeded with profit) was look'd upon with an ill Eie, their Neighbours did scorne to follow it, though not to do it was to their own detriment.'[13] Many improvements in farming methods required capital beyond the financial resources of small cultivators; other developments involved the reorganisation of the common fields, and farmers were understandably suspicious of proposals that threatened their rights in the arable fields or on the commons. Some techniques were suited only to certain types of soil or particular topographies; some experiments, such as the draining of fens and marshes, were not always successful. In many cases poor communications prevented the spread of knowledge of new methods. Thus progress in agriculture spread slowly, and a great deal of farming in the late eighteenth century was little altered from the methods employed two centuries earlier.

It is not surprising, therefore, that until the mid-seventeenth century at least, in the race between increasing population and increasing food supplies, the former was the hare and the latter the tortoise. The clearest evidence for this is the rise in grain prices. By the 1640s they were seven times higher than their level of the early sixteenth century; animal and animal product prices had also risen to a slightly lesser extent. Not all the increase was caused by the demand for food outstripping supply. It was partly the result of a fall in the value of money which had been caused by an increase in the supply of financial resources; and at various times in the sixteenth and early seventeenth centuries increasing expenditure by the government had contributed to inflation. Some part of the enhanced prices of agricultural produce, too, must be attributed to rising costs of distribution, for the number of people who were buying their food in the markets rather than from the farms was constantly increasing. Nevertheless, agricultural prices rose more sharply than prices in general between 1500 and 1650, suggesting that the expansion of agricultural production failed to keep pace with the growth of population. Prices also rose by more than the money incomes of wage-earners, whose purchasing power was therefore sharply reduced. By the 1630s or 1640s wage-earners enjoyed less than half the real income of their counterparts at the beginning of the sixteenth century. Since the proportion of people depending on money wages had been growing in the period, a large and increasing section of the population of Tudor and early Stuart England were suffering from falling standards of consumption.

Conditions improved somewhat during the second half of the seventeenth century when the tortoise of agricultural progress edged ahead of the hare of population— indeed, the hare was taking a rest, for, as we have already noticed, the growth of population in England slackened in the second half of the seventeenth century. From the 1660s the trend of grain prices was gradually downward, although the fall was punctuated by short periods of rising prices. Pastoral product prices remained more buoyant, because the demand pattern switched to meat and dairy products as bread became cheaper. English agriculture even began to produce a surplus of corn for export for the first time since the sixteenth century, and in the early eighteenth century grain came to be an important item in overseas trade. By the eighteenth century also, money wages were rising and the diets of labourers improved. The poor abandoned their brown rye and barley bread for loaves of white wheaten flour; they also ate more fruit and vegetables. 'It is well known', wrote Joseph Massie in 1757, 'that *Gardening* hath much improved in this kingdom, within fifty years last past, and that vastly greater Quantities of Roots, Fruits, and Greens, such as *Turnips, Potatoes, Cabbages, Colliflowers*, etc., have been grown of *late Years*.'[14] Not only home-grown food but imported luxuries were consumed among the lower classes. In Nottingham in the 1740s they were buying 'Sugars, Spices and all sorts of Grocers Goods, almost as cheap as in London. . . . Every Seamer, Sizer, and Winder will have her Tea and will enjoy herself over it in a morning, not forgetting their Snuff . . . and even a common washer-woman thinks she has not had a proper Breakfast without tea and hot buttered white Bread.'[15]

According to Gregory King, writing at the end of the seventeenth century, just over half of the population received yearly incomes that did not cover their yearly expenses. It was this stratum of the population that was particularly susceptible to the state of the harvests. It does not follow, however, that pre-industrial Englishmen commonly faced starvation because up to half the population was worse fed in the mid-seventeenth century than their predecessors had been in 1500: Englishmen were relatively well-fed at the beginning of the sixteenth century. Famine was not a regular feature of pre-industrial England; but hunger was a recurrent visitor, coming and going with the seasons, and sometimes settling in for a protracted stay. It frequently appeared in late winter and

early spring when the barns were bare and the last slices
had been cut from the salt bacon hanging from the raf-
ters; it retreated as the summer brought the fruit and
grain harvests. If the harvest was good, there was plenty
of corn to be put in store, meal and flour were cheap in
the markets, brewers and distillers had plenty of raw
materials, and animal feed was plentiful. Conversely, a
poor harvest caused a shortage of food for man and beast.
On average, one harvest in four or five was poor in the
sixteenth  and seventeenth centuries, and bad seasons
tended to be bunched, two or three occurring in successive
years. This was because an initial poor crop caused a
shortfall in seed corn which led to a depleted harvest in
the following season. It took a good year of favourable
weather to break out of the cycle. On the other hand, two
or three good years running together created abundance,
leading farmers to bewail the horrors of plenty as corn
prices fell until checked by a turn in the weather.

With the fluctuations of the seasons there must have
been many hungry periods in English history, made all
the more severe by poor transport that prevented shortages in one locality from being remedied by surpluses from
another. Some years stand out as particularly famished
periods in pre-industrial England. As we have seen, population was growing during the first half of the sixteenth
century, and by the middle of the century food supplies
had become very tight. In the late 1540s and early 1550s
a series of crop failures led to a crisis of subsistence. Between 1549 and 1556 there was not a single good harvest,
those of 1555 and 1556 being especially bad. In 1549 grain
prices were 84 per cent higher than prices in the previous
year, and in 1556 they were 240 per cent higher. There
were complaints of hardship on all sides, all the more
strident since the export trade was depressed, and so money
incomes were reduced at the same time as the cost of food
was increasing. As prices rose, so did tempers. In 1551 an
unfortunate baker in Norwich was attacked by 'dyvers

folk being in his bakehouse . . . [who] had communication upon the great prises of grayn and victuelle'.[16] The food problem was especially acute in the towns; and Worcester was only one of several cities whose authorities bought corn for sale to their citizens. In 1556–57 the Worcester corporation purchased £133 worth of rye 'for the relief of the poor within our city, being a godly purpose and godly mission'.[17] On a wider front, the Privy Council prohibited the export of corn in every year between 1546 and 1550.

This particular crisis passed, partly because high death rates during the 1550s and early 1560s reduced the pressure on food supplies, and partly because of the return of better weather. There is little evidence of acute hunger on a wide scale for the next couple of decades, but near-famine conditions were widespread in 1586–87, when there was one bad and one very bad harvest; in the north-west of the country a few people may actually have died of starvation. In the early 1590s, by contrast, a run of good harvests so reduced the price of corn that in 1593 the government repealed legislation designed to check the movement of tillage land into pasture. But the very next year saw the first of four bad harvests, followed by two rather ordinary seasons. These were near-famine years. The city of Worcester spent £1,800 (an enormous sum for the time) on Baltic grain which was sold below cost price. At Salisbury the authorities bought imported grain from merchants in Southampton to 'pacyfie the great outcry of the poor'.[18] Even so, burials in the town in 1597 were twice their usual level. Perhaps the population had been swollen by the large numbers of migrants attracted into the city in the hope of getting food: ninety-six vagrants were whipped out of the city in 1598. In Bristol a city alderman spent £1,200 of his own to provide grain for the poor; and the city of Norwich also sold corn below cost. The distress was particularly acute in the north. At Newcastle in 1597 'sundrie [were] starving and

dying in our streets and in the fields for lack of bread';
and in September and October of that year the city
buried twenty-five 'poor folkes who died for want in the
streets'. Throughout Cumberland and Westmorland in
1596 and 1597 mortality ran at high levels because of the
'great dearth and famyn wherewith the country hath
been punished extreamelie theis three hard yeares by
past'.[19] In 1598 the magistrates at Leeds recorded the
death of a woman who came to the town begging and 'did
fall extreamely sicke', leaving a young child 'not past a
yeare old' which the town was 'far unable to releive ... by
reason they are alreadie overcharged with their owne
poore'.

These dreadful years provoked widespread despair and
anxiety. They formed the basis of Titania's description of
famine in *A Midsummer Night's Dream*, written about
1596:

> Therefore the winds, piping to us in vain,
> As in revenge, have suck'd up from the sea
> Contagious fogs; which falling in the land,
> Hath every pelting river made so proud,
> That they have overcome their continents:
> The ox hath therefore stretch'd his yoke in vain,
> The ploughman lost his sweat; and the green corn
> Hath rotted ere his youth attain'd a beard:
> The fold stands empty in the drowned field,
> And crows are fatted with the murrion flock. . . .
> The human mortals want their winter cheer;
> No night is now with hymn or carol blest:
> Therefore the moon, the governess of floods,
> Pale in her anger, washes all the air,
> That rheumatic diseases do abound:
> And through this distemperature we see
> The seasons alter: hoary-headed frosts
> Fall in the fresh lap of the crimson rose;
> And on old Hiems' chin and icy crown

An odorous chaplet of sweet summer buds
Is, as in mockery, set: the spring, the summer,
The childing autumn, angry winter, change
Their wonted liveries; and the mazed world,
By their increase, now knows not which is which.[20]

More prosaically, a provincial justice, alarmed by food
riots and other disturbances, wrote to the Privy Council
that seditious men were abroad, stirring up trouble 'in
this time of dearthe, who no dowpt anymate [men] to all
contempte both of noblemen and gentlemen, contynually
bussynge into their eares that the ritche men have gotten
all into ther hands and will starve the poore'. The root of
the problem, thought the justice, were 'the infynyte numbers of idle wandrynge people and robbers of the land', so
many that 'ther ar scant sufficient to do the ordinary
tyllage of the land'. But, he continued, normal punishment would only worsen matters, for if these 'lewde
people are comytted to the gayle the poor country
[people] . . . are inforced there to feede them, which they
greve'.[21] The increase in the numbers of wandering people
at this time was in fact a symptom of widespread distress,
not the cause. As food prices soared, unemployment increased because the demand for all goods except the
essentials of life fell, and men and women roamed the
countryside in search of food and jobs. The government
acted with vigour against the rising tide of paupers and
vagabonds. During 1597 the House of Commons debated
thirteen bills concerning pauperism and vagabondage.
The product of these discussions was the great Tudor Poor
Law which, modified in 1601, remained the basis of
English social legislation until 1834. Rogues, beggars and
vagabonds were to be punished, the sick cared for, and
the jobless put to work.

In 1607 and 1608 there were anti-enclosure riots in the
Midlands sparked off by locally high prices. On the whole,
though, the early seventeenth century was not a period of

acute scarcity, and in 1620–21 landowners were taking a jaundiced view of low grain prices:

> The rates of all sorts of corn were so extremely low as it made the very prices of land fall from twenty years' purchase to sixteen or seventeen. . . . All farmers generally murmured at this plenty and cheapness; and the poorer sort that would have been glad but a few years before of the coarse rye-bread did now, usually, traverse the markets to find out the finer wheats, as if nothing else would serve their use or please their palates.[22]

But within two years England was gripped in hunger, even though prices did not rise to the disastrous levels of 1596. Reports of near-famine and starvation were widespread. In Lincolnshire, a fertile region,

> There are many thousands . . . who have sold all they have even to their bedstraw, and cannot get work to earn any money. Dog's flesh is a dainty dish, and found upon search in many houses, also such horse flesh as hath lain long in a dike for hounds, and the other day one stole a sheep, who for mere hunger tore a leg out, and yet the great time of scarcity not yet come.[23]

At Greystoke in Cumberland the parish register for 1623 chronicled a pathetic procession of the famished to the graveyard. In January 'a poor fellow destitute of succour was brought out of the street' and died in the house of the village constable. In March Dorothy, 'a poor hunger-starved beggar child', was buried, together with Thomas Simpson, 'a poor hunger-starved beggar boy' who had wandered from Brough in Westmorland, twenty-five miles away. In May 'James Irwin, a poor beggar strippling born upon the borders of England . . . died . . . in great misery' and was added to the bony collection in the cemetery. They were joined in July by the infant Thomas Bell who 'died for very want of food and maintenance to live'. And so it went on, even through the harvest months. A widow and her son died in a barn on 11 and 12 September 'for want of food and maintenance to live'. So too did the four-year-old son of John Lancaster at the end of the month, and the child's mother a week later. Another child starved to death at the end of October while his father 'went forth out of the country for want of means'.[24] Further south things were not much better. At Salisbury the poor 'were like Pharaoh's leane Kine, even ready to eat up the fat ones'.[25] As in the 1550s, the suffering caused by the high prices of food was made worse by a severe slump in the export trade in woollen cloth. This caused widespread unemployment since many people earned their living making or selling cloth. The balance of payments deteriorated because of the collapse of the cloth export trade, and money flowed out of the country, leading to deflation, which further aggravated the economic difficulties of the time.

There was little immediate relief, although starvation on the scale of 1623 did not recur. Corn prices fell in the mid-1620s but rose again at the end of the decade and in the 1630s twice reached the famine levels of 1596. Taking the 1620s and 1630s together, there had probably never been a worse time in English history for wage-earners. There was some respite in the 1640s, although dearth returned in 1647–49. But the abyss was beginning to recede as the slackening of population growth made it less likely that a bad season or two would push the country to the edge of famine. Hunger still pinched from time to time, notably in the 1690s and more severely in 1709–10, when much of Europe was afflicted by dearth. The winter of 1708–09 was hard, with a long frost from October to March and virtually no growth of crops until May. Grain prices soared: at Michaelmas 1708 wheat had sold in Cambridge for twenty-nine shillings a quarter; in 1709 the price was eighty shillings, and sixty shillings the following year in spite of a better harvest. Not only corn, but meat and dairy produce was expensive because of the shortage of animal feed. Food riots broke out in various parts of the country and the death rate rose: in London, 16,100 deaths had occurred in the year October 1706 to September 1707; in 1709–10 the figure was 24,700.

Another subsistence crisis occurred in 1727–30, when the harvests were again adversely affected by bad weather. Throughout England generally death rates were higher than birth rates, and in some parts of the Midlands mortality was two or three times higher than normal. There were some cases of actual starvation, perhaps for the last time in England. A Yorkshire doctor reported in 1727 that 'Many of the labouring and poor people, who used a low diet, and were much exposed to the injuries and changes of the weather, died; many of whom probably wanted the necessary assistance of diet and medicines. . . . Many of the little country towns and villages were stripped of people.'[26] There were corn riots in Cornwall and Wales, and grain was imported from Europe to make up shortage in home supplies. Hardship returned in 1740 following another harsh winter when 'an unheard of frost seized with extraordinary severity on the world and the elements'. The cold continued into the spring, and the weather remained unseasonable throughout the summer so that 'the harvest was not over till late in the autumn, and by the middle of October the frost returned before the fruit in the gardens had had time to ripen'. Food was scarce and the poor 'unable to sustain oppressive want and hunger's urgent pain'.[27] Mortality rose in the towns when people, weakened by hunger, succumbed to disease. But the crisis was quickly over, and in the ensuing years less was heard of dearth, in spite of the increase in the population that had been taking place from the 1740s. It was symptomatic of the improvement in standards of consumption which had occurred over the previous decades that when severe weather in 1795 forced wheat prices up to their highest levels since 1709, triggering off food riots in many parts of the country, the poor obstinately stuck to their diets of white wheaten bread, washed down with tea and sugar.

If famine was rarely a direct cause of death in pre-industrial England, how then did diet contribute to the high death rates of the time? The cereal-based diets eaten by the bulk of the population needed supplementing by dairy products, meat, fruit and vegetables. Without sufficient 'white meats'—butter, cheese and eggs—there was a risk of vitamin A deficiencies, causing eye disorders, skin eruptions, and 'a weakening of the defences of the body against invasion of bacteria and other disease-producing organisms'.[28] The author of *The Decaye of England Only by the Great Multitude of Shepe*, written between 1550 and 1553, complained that 'the more shepe, the skanter is the white meat', and 'the fewer egges for a peny'.[29] In winter these things were always in short supply; and with the loss of commons and the gradual alienation of the population from the land it is likely that supplies became more uncertain for many people. In time of dearth, shortages of grain may also have led to vitamin B deficiencies which could cause skin disorders and—in extreme cases—pellagra. More widespread deficiency diseases were scurvy and rickets, resulting from lack of vitamins C and D. With repeated periods of food shortage, these conditions were common and, although they did not directly cause death, they rendered the population prone to infection from more lethal illnesses.

The condition of food also contributed to disease and mortality. Much of it was tainted. In the nineteenth century, for example, milk was a common source of tuberculosis, a disease which was also very common in earlier periods and probably arose from much the same source. Milk was not regarded as particularly good for adults in the seventeenth and eighteenth centuries, with good reason, given the state in which it was sold in the towns, from open pails 'exposed to foul rinsings discharged from doors and windows, spittle, snot, and tobacco quids, from foot passengers'. Similarly, meat was fly-blown and tainted; grain, meal and flour were dirty and frequently adulterated. Inevitably, food that was sold in weekly markets and from 'moveable shops that run upon wheels, attended by ill-looking fellows',[30] in an age that did not recognise the possibilities of contamination, was the source of many intestinal disorders. So too was the water supply, which was generally drawn from the same sources as water used for washing, for industry, and the disposal of sewerage. When food was scarce the dangers of eating totally unsuitable foods increased considerably. Acorns and tares were used to eke out grain, and even more extreme measures were resorted to. The 'witch of famine', as Thomas Dekker put it, 'makest men eate slovenly, and feede on excrements of Beasts, and at one meale Swallow a hundred pound in very Doves-dung'.[31]

Hunger also sent men on the move. As we have observed, the problem of vagabondage increased in times of scarcity. According to contemporaries, vagabonds 'be generally given to horrible uncleanness, they have not particular wives, neither do they range themselves into Families: but consent together as beasts'. They were the means by which infectious diseases spread from one part of the country to another; and since many of them flocked to the towns in search of food and employment, they added to the congestion there and to the likelihood of the spread of crowd infections such as plague and typhus.

Periodic shortages of food had other, less obvious, effects on the size of population in pre-industrial England. For example, malnutrition reduced the number of conceptions by interrupting the menstrual cycle of ill-nourished women. And when hunger was accompanied by heavy mortality, the number of marriages fell, both because of the death of prospective marriage partners and because marriages were put off until the return of better times. When there was a sequence of harvest failures or mortality crises, it was possible for society as a whole in some mysterious fashion to change its habits so that marriages were regularly contracted at a later age and the number of children born to a marriage reduced. Something like this seems to have occurred in the mid-seventeenth century, with the result that in the second half of the century fertility was lower compared to the levels of the sixteenth and early seventeenth centuries. Thus the Malthusian spectre, of population remorselessly increasing up to and beyond the levels of food supplies, was avoided.

In another way, too, the Malthusian connection between population growth, food supplies, disease and mortality was not always valid. Although periods of bad harvests frequently led to high mortality, times of high mortality did not always coincide with times of bad harvests. For example, the late 1550s were sickly years, even though the harvest failures of the earlier part of the decade were over and food prices were falling. More generally, the second half of the seventeenth century seems to have been more unhealthy than the first half, despite the fact that food supplies were normally easier and grain prices were not rising. Similarly, the two decades 1730–50 were generally a period of good harvests and cheap grain—the year 1740 was a glaring exception. Yet in many of these years the death rate was above the birth rate throughout the country. Some diseases, it seems, had a life cycle of their own, regardless of the state of food supplies. If they broke out in times of dearth, their consequences were all the more deadly for they were able to harvest their victims from an undernourished population. But their onset was not determined by the state of the harvest. Disease and dearth were sometimes independent threats to the lives of Englishmen before the Industrial Revolution.

## 3
## 'From Winter, Plague and Pestilence, Good Lord, Deliver Us'

MANY battalions marched in the army of death. Hunger was its artillery, grumbling intermittently through the seasons, wearing down the enemy, and spasmodically erupting into a great barrage of near-famine. The infantry was the myriad of illnesses that was always present in the community. These included the deficiency diseases such as scurvy, pellagra and rickets. According to one medical authority, 'most of the poorer population [of Tudor England] were probably in a condition of sub-clinical scurvy after their winter diet of salt bacon, bread, and peas'.[1] Pellagra is caused by a shortage of vitamin B and affects the skin and nervous system; it is found today among maize-eating communities. It is not clear whether it was ever widespread in countries such as England that consumed wheat, rye and barley; but it is possible that some of the references at the end of the fifteenth century to leprosy in England may, in fact, indicate pellagra, since the two diseases have a superficial resemblance. There is no doubt at all about the presence of rickets, although the first English description of the disease was not written until 1645 under the title *On the Disease of English Children which in their Language is called the Rickets.*

An extremely common illness was tuberculosis. In the seventeenth and eighteenth centuries it was responsible for about one-fifth of all deaths in London, except during years when epidemics of plague raged. It was particularly severe on children under fourteen. The population was also scourged by rheumatism, arthritis and gout. The

upper ranks of society were much troubled by kidney and
bladder stones caused by diets that were deficient in milk
and butter. Before the mid-seventeenth century, at least
one in twelve of the English aristocracy endured the
anguish of the stone. Measles, chicken-pox, mumps,
whooping-cough, sore throats and the common cold afflicted rich and poor alike, virtually without challenge from
medical science. Queen Elizabeth and Sir William Cecil,
her chief minister, suffered miserably at Christmas 1563.

> The cold here hath so assayled us [reported Cecil] that
> the Queen's majestie hath been much troubled, and is
> not yet free of the same that I had in November, which
> they call a pooss [i.e. a cough], and now this Christmas,
> to keep her Majestie company, I have been newly so
> possessed with it as I could not see, but with some ado
> I wryte this.[2]

If the chill could penetrate the fires and furs of Westminster Palace, how much more easily could it intrude
through the daub and thatch of peasant cottages.

To the steady miseries of coughs, sores, aches, and
itches were added the devastations of the panzer divisions
of epidemic diseases, those 'Cowards of Hell, that strike
in peace, when the whole worlds unarmede: Tripping
up soules of Beggars, limblesse wretches, Hole-stopping
prisoners, miserable catchpoles. . . .'[3] Two of the most
deadly were bubonic plague and typhus, both of which
were endemic among rat populations and sometimes
spilled over into the neighbouring human population with
catastrophic consequences. Another killer was influenza
which, in conjunction with pneumonia, was apt to explode
into a frenzy of rapid activity, race through the population, and subside as suddenly as it came. Dysentery—the
'bloody flux'—and allied intestinal disorders were always
present in the insanitary conditions of the time, and they
periodically swelled to epidemic proportions, especially in
summer. Syphilis was recruited to the ranks of epidemics

at the end of the fifteenth century and ran a virulent course until about 1600, when it settled down into an endemic risk attending dissolute living. Smallpox, on the other hand, was an old-established disease, but it assumed a major epidemic form mainly during the seventeenth and early eighteenth centuries.

It is not easy to apportion blame for heavy mortality in pre-industrial England to one epidemic disease rather than another, since contemporaries rarely distinguished clearly between them. Some diseases, indeed, shared similar characteristics, at least in their early stages. Typhus, for example, could be mistaken for influenza in its early stages and manifested many forms, accounting for the many names by which it has been known in the past. The word 'fever' was used indiscriminately to describe all febrile conditions before the nineteenth century and was no more precise than 'cancer' is today. Most observers in the sixteenth and seventeenth centuries, however, were able to recognise an epidemic of bubonic plague, the most spectacular, if not the most common, cause of death until the third quarter of the seventeenth century. Its distinctive swelling and discolouring of the glands in the groin, neck and armpits, its predilection for hot summer weather, and its fatality rate made plague recognisable and fearful. Even so, it was sometimes confused with 'spotted fever', a name commonly given to typhus, and not all commentators were prepared to check the clinical symptoms carefully before labelling any lethal outbreak of illness as plague. Thus bubonic plague has gained a notoriety among historians and been credited with causing more deaths than it deserves and has obscured the importance of other diseases in causing the high mortality prevalent in pre-industrial England.

The nearest we can get to a statistical estimation of the mortality rates of various illnesses comes from the London Bills of Mortality, which were weekly totals of burials occurring in London parishes and kept from about 1529.

During the seventeenth century they became increasingly specific about causes of death, although it has to be remembered that the accuracy of the observations of those who compiled the bills, and the nature of the descriptions, were not always very good. It must also be borne in mind that London was an untypical community in pre-industrial England and its pattern of mortality may have been different to that of the country as a whole. During the years 1661–86 almost 600,000 burials were recorded in London. In nearly 40 per cent of the cases the cause of death was attributed to plague, 'fever and spotted fever', smallpox, measles, or 'griping of the guts'. Plague itself accounted for just under 12 per cent of burials, followed by fevers, including 'spotted fever' (i.e. typhus), and 'griping of the guts' (i.e. dysentery), each with about 10 per cent. Smallpox had 34,000 victims, and the rest were a long way behind. Included in this period were 1665 and 1666, when plague deaths were very numerous. If these years are excluded, total deaths fall to 518,000 and plague deaths to a mere 128. In non-plague years typhus and dysentery were the most important epidemics, although together they accounted for only 28 per cent of total mortality. The bulk of deaths were caused by ailments always in attendance, such as tuberculosis, the illnesses of childhood and the diseases of old age.

In any discussions of epidemic disease plague requires a chapter to itself because of the special place it holds in the history of mortality. It has overshadowed typhus in importance, although the former was more constant in its attentions and probably responsible for some of the deaths commonly attributed to plague. In only two years between 1661 and 1686 did fever and spotted fever deaths in London fall below a thousand, and in seventeen years they were over two thousand. 'Typhus is an acute fever which does not always behave in a conventional manner.' Initially it was marked by a high temperature and displayed symptoms similar to influenza, but within four or five days the patient usually broke out in a pink rash which later turned purple or brown and was the reason for its popular name of 'spotted fever'. The sufferer endured severe headaches before lapsing into delirium and ultimately into death. Typhus typically occurred in wretched, overcrowded conditions, as may be guessed from its other common names, which included camp, prison, and ship fever. Andrew Boorde, the first physician to write a medical book in England (in 1547) and who himself died of the disease, described typhus as

> the sycknesse of the prisons. This infirmitie doth come out of the corruption of the ayre, and the breath and fylth the which doth come from men, as many men are to be together in a lyttle room having but lyttle open ayre. The chief remedy is for men so to live, and so to do, that he desearve not to be brought into no prison. And if he be in prison eyther to get friendes to helpe hym out, or else to use some perfumes . . . and to keep the prison clene.[4]

Typhus originated among rats but the organism responsible for it was transmitted from rat to rat and from rats to men by fleas and lice. Once established in the human population, it was carried from man to man by lice. The widespread presence of typhus in pre-industrial England testifies to the lousiness of the age. Following the murder of Thomas Becket in 1170, it was reported that the lice flowed from the seven layers of clothing surrounding his chilling body like water boiling over a simmering cauldron. Neither standards of cleanliness nor quantities of clothing had changed much by Tudor times. Among the upper classes, fashion and draughty manor-houses alike obliged the wearing of large amounts of heavy clothing; and among the labouring poor, garments made from coarse woollens were ill-suited to washing. In Restoration London Pepys reported his visits to the barber to have his wig 'cleansed of its nits' as freely as a twentieth-century diarist might record a visit to the hairdresser. On one occasion his wife cut his hair and 'found in my head and body about twenty lice, little and big'.[5] Little thought was given to lice, apart from their irritating presence, for the connection between them and typhus was not appreciated until the twentieth century.

The incidence of typhus before the sixteenth century is not clear, but it has been suggested that it reached epidemic proportions in Europe only at the end of the fifteenth century. In England it made a number of dramatic appearances at a series of so-called 'black assizes' at Cambridge in 1522, Oxford in 1577, and Exeter in 1586, in which the infection spread from the jails to judges and juries, and so to the population at large. At Exeter, for example, 'There happened a verie sudden and strange sicknesse, first among the prisoners of the Gaole and Castell of Exon, and then dispersed (upon their triall) amongst sundrie other persons.' The disease was supposed to have originated among Portuguese seamen taken from a prize ship who were lodged at Exeter castle:

> These men had beene before a long time at the seas, and had no change of apparell, nor laine in bed, and noe lieing upon the ground without succor or reliefe, were soon infected . . . and this sicknesse verie soone after dispersed itselfe amoung the residue of the prisoners . . . of which disease manie of them died, but all brought into great extremities and were hardly escaped. These men, when they were to be brought before the . . . justices for their triall, manie of them were so weak and sicke that they were not able to goe or stande ; but were carried from the gaole to the place of judgement, some upon hand barrowes, and some between men leading them.[6]

The movement of paupers, vagabonds and beggars, arising from the growth of population and the periodic failures of the harvest during the sixteenth century, helped to spread typhus throughout the country. Small localised epidemics broke out spasmodically, particularly in winter and years of scarcity. Typhus was mainly a winter illness, for it was then that clothes remained unchanged and unwashed, and men—and rats—huddled in households for warmth and shelter. Then the lice could commute easily from person to person. The association between typhus and food shortages was recognised in another of its names: 'famine fever'. In times of extreme scarcity the disease seems to have taken particular hold among rats and men alike. As infected rats died lice and fleas abandoned their dead hosts for human ones, thus spreading infection among an undernourished population. Typhus may well have been present in many places in England during the hungry 1550s; and there is strong evidence that it contributed to the high mortality in the north-west during the famine years of 1586–87. It was at work again in the early 1620s when it broke out in Scotland and along the Border and was reported in London at the end of 1623 where it 'hath carried away many of the good sort, as well as meaner people'.[7] London continued feverish throughout 1624, whether from typhus or influenza is unclear, but the infection was obliterated by a severe epidemic of plague in 1625.

By about the middle of the seventeenth century fevers of the typhus type—it is not always possible to distinguish between one fever and another in contemporary descriptions—had become well established as more or less regular visitors in England causing more deaths, year in and year out, than plague. The increasingly endemic nature of typhus is perhaps one explanation of the greater unhealthiness of England in the later seventeenth and early eighteenth centuries. In 1643 a physician with the Royalist army at Oxford described typhus as the 'new disease'. It attracted attention to itself at that time by the impartiality with which it fought for both Royalist and Parliamentary armies. In early 1643 a Royalist force was besieged at Reading by 5,000 infantry and 3,000 cavalry. When the town fell in April the Parliamentary army found that many of the defenders had died of sickness. Meanwhile the King's army had withdrawn to Oxford,

> where at first the soldiers, being disposed in the open fields, and afterwards among the towns and villages, suffered not much less. For the foot [soldiers] being pact together in close houses, when they had filled all things with filthiness and unwholesome nastiness and stinking odours . . . they fell sick by troops, and as it were by squadrons.[8]

The two armies chased one another into the West Country, taking infection with them. Both were in Tiverton in the autumn of 1644, and the town was struck by disease, probably typhus, causing many deaths. In October 105 people were buried in the town, compared with a normal monthly total of between twelve and fifteen; in all as many as ten or twelve per cent of the population died of the epidemic.

In post-Restoration England typhus fever was practically a part of everyday life. Ever present on a small scale, it sometimes flared up to epidemic proportions, as, for example, in the late 1690s, 1709–10, 1718–19, the late 1720s and 1741–42, all periods following poor harvests. In the last of these years typhus was at least partly responsible for a death rate of nearly eighty per thousand in Nottingham between March 1741 and March 1742, well over double the worst rates found in the nineteenth-century industrial city. In 1750 there was a repetition of the earlier black assizes in London, when typhus broke out at the Old Bailey, killing two judges, the lord mayor, an alderman, a barrister, two or three law students, two court officials, several jurors, and 'about forty other persons whose business or curiosity had brought them hither'.[9] On the whole, however, during the eighteenth century typhus settled down into an endemic but not highly virulent disease, killing perhaps one-tenth of its victims and found mainly in the poorest, most congested parts of towns. Somewhat surprisingly, its incidence declined with the onset of industrialisation and the growth of manufacturing towns. It occasionally swelled to epidemic proportions in the nineteenth century, notably in 1815 and 1847–48, but it was losing ground as a cause of death to enteric fevers of one sort or another. At the end of the nineteenth century, when the cause of typhus was not yet understood, a distinguished medical historian could write that 'The disappearance, during the last twenty years, of typhus . . . is one of the most certain and striking facts in our epidemiology.'[10]

Typhus was only one of many feverish conditions that afflicted pre-industrial Englishmen. Many of them were very mild, like the one that caused the servant of the Earl of Cardigan to take to his bed in November 1725: 'He has a fever upon him, but is something better since he has been blooded.' A year later the Earl's housekeeper suffered from a fever that 'hangs upon her still, but not in a violent manner'. Even more benevolent was 'the swet' taken one night by his lordship's steward 'which I believe did me good'.[11] These were vague, inconsequential ailments, common enough in our own day.

There were, however, at least two other fevers that affected pre-industrial England from time to time in a more dynamic fashion. One, influenza, is still present today in various forms; the other, malaria, had passed off the medical map of England by the early nineteenth century. Neither name is particularly helpful in tracing the history of these infections. Both are Italian in origin and both date from the eighteenth century. Both names, too, echo an early theory of infection that explained diseases as arising from the baleful influences of earthly or astrological bodies. Influenza was thought to be an infection caused by hostile planets or comets; malaria was a disease caused by bad air. Severe epidemics of influenza swept through England on several occasions in the sixteenth, seventeenth and eighteenth centuries. The 'English sweat' of the early sixteenth century was probably a form of influenza, although medical historians are not all agreed on this. It made a spectacular progress through early Tudor England, appearing at the Battle of Bosworth and accompanying the new king Henry VII to London, where it killed several leading citizens and caused the postponement of the coronation. It turned up again in 1508 and in 1517, when it was blamed for the deaths of four hundred students at Oxford. An outbreak in London in 1528 was said to have affected 40,000—the bulk of the population if the report be true—although only 2,000 of them died. In 1551 the sweat appeared so quickly in so many places that it was christened by a clergyman 'the Posting-Sweat, that posted from town to town thorow England and was named the "Stop-gallant" for it spared none. For there were some dancing in the Court at nine o'clock that were dead at eleven."[12] Among these outbreaks of the sweat were some clearly distinguishable waves of influenza, including a European epidemic in 1510 that spread into England and a severe epidemic in 1556 and 1557 that returned with renewed vigour in 1558.

What diseases and sicknesses everywhere prevailed! the like whereof had never been known before, both for the lasting and the mortality of them: which being hot burning fevers and other strange diseases, began in the great dearth 1556, and increased more and more the two following years. In the Summer 1557 they raged horribly throughout the realm and killed an exceeding number of all sorts of men, but especially gentlemen and men of great wealth. So many husbandmen and labourers also died. . . . In the latter end of the year, quartan agues were so common among men, women, and young children also, that few houses escaped. . . . In 1558 . . . about August, the same fevers raged again in such manner, as never plague or pestilence . . . killed a greater number. If the people of the realm had been divided into four parts, certainly three parts of those four should have been found sick. . . . The winter following, also, the quartan agues continued in like manner, or more vehemently than they had done last year.[13]

The reference in this contemporary description to the high mortality accompanying the outbreak suggests that typhus or some other disease was at work with influenza.

The influenza outbreak of the 1550s contributed to the deaths of up to one-fifth of the population in some parts of the country. No other epidemic in the sixteenth or early seventeenth century has attracted so much attention. In October 1675 the diarist John Evelyn recorded that he 'got an extreme cold, such as was afterwards so epidemical, as not only to afflict us in this island, but was rife over all Europe like a plague'.[14] There was a major outbreak of influenza in 1729, and again in 1733, 1737 and 1743. This last epidemic was the first to be described by contemporaries as influenza. It arrived in England from Europe in February and was in London a month later. Writing in March 1743, Horace Walpole declared:

It is a cold and a fever. I had one of the worst and was blooded on Saturday and Sunday, but it is quite gone; my father was blooded last night; his is but slight. . . . Our army abroad would shudder to see what streams of blood have been let out! Nobody has died of it . . . but old Mr Eyres of Chelsea, through obstancy of not bleeding, and his ancient Grace [Archbishop] of York; Wilcox of Rochester succeeds him, who is fit for nothing in the world but to die of this cold too.[15]

The death rate throughout London trebled at the height of the epidemic, although the new Archbishop of York managed to survive.

In the low-lying fens and marshes of pre-industrial

England lurked malaria, less as an epidemic than as a constant companion, like the mists and fogs that rose from the watery wastes. To contemporaries malaria was generally known as ague, qualified by such adjectives as tertian, quartan, etc., indicating the frequency of the paroxysms. The term ague, like fever, was not used with precision, and not all historians accept the identification of malaria with ague, although, on balance, ague does seem to have been a malarial infection. It was probably malaria that interrupted the studies at Cambridge of William Harvey, the physician, in 1598 and 1599. The disease was still prevalent in the nineteenth century, particularly in the East Anglian fens, Romney and Pevensey marshes, and the low-lying land around the Thames estuary. In the 1850s malaria cases treated in St Thomas's Hospital in London averaged five per cent of all patients. In the light of this evidence we can more readily accept, as Defoe did, tales of the high mortality caused by agues in the Essex marshes in the 1720s. At the time Defoe wrote the average life expectancy at birth in the fenland village of Wrangle was fourteen years, compared with about thirty-five for England as a whole; sixty per cent of the inhabitants of the village died before the age of twenty-one. Even in the generally unhealthy context of pre-industrial England, the fens and marshes were exceptionally dangerous; they were undoubtedly a good deal more deadly than the industrial towns of the nineteenth century. As the marshes were effectively drained in the nineteenth century malaria disappeared as an important cause of death in England.

There is a school of romantic thought that regards the Industrial Revolution as bringing disaster to the working classes in England by creating a rigid discipline of factory work and destroying a simple mode of rural life. Part of this simple life was simple sanitation that provided the conditions in which dysentery could flourish. Dysentery was known variously as bloody flux, lusk, surfeit, griping of the guts, and summer or infantile diarrhoea. Far from being a creation of nineteenth-century urban society, alimentary ailments were as common as fresh air in pre-industrial England and as much a part of the country scene as ploughing and harvest. In London and the provincial towns dysentery was a regular summer visitor, and was an important cause of death among children. 'From the middle of July to the middle of September', wrote a doctor in 1689, 'these epidemic gripes of infants are so common (being the annual heat of the season doth entirely exhaust their strength) that more infants, affected with these, do die in one month than in another three that are gentle.'[16] Adults were also affected, although with less deadly consequences than for children. In 1540, for example, England was gripped by a 'great lusk throughout the realm'; and dysentery was part of the widespread blanket of sickness that wrapped the realm during the 1550s. It was an important cause of death during the near-famine years of the late 1590s; in 1596, for example, nineteen out of twenty-eight burials in Finchley churchyard were of victims of dysentery, and in the following year twenty-three out of twenty-eight. Like typhus, dysentery was a scourge of armies and ships, and it inflicted more casualties on the English fleet after the defeat of the Armada than the Spanish achieved in the pursuit of 'God's enterprise'.

The clearest evidence of the ravages of dysentery comes from the London Bills of Mortality. Admittedly the metropolis, 'where houses thick and sewers annoy the air', was not a typical community. Ninety per cent of the population of England lived in villages and towns of less than 30,000 inhabitants in the late seventeenth century, not in cities half a million strong. Nevertheless, more than ten per cent of all deaths in England took place in London and its suburbs, and all communities, both urban and rural, suffered from water-borne infections. In London during the years 1667–1720, that is, after the final outbreak of plague, deaths from intestinal infections accounted for between one-fifth and one-third of all deaths. They were highest among infants, infantile diarrhoea being probably the most common single cause of deaths among babies. Older children and adults, apart from the elderly, often recovered from attacks, although they were left weakened and prone to other diseases. Dysentery among adults may have become less common during the eighteenth century, but it remained widespread among children. In the nineteenth century a new twist was given to this noisome area of population history by the introduction of Asiatic cholera into the factory towns.

Two other diseases among the dismal catalogue of human affliction have attracted more attention from historians than dysentery: the poxes, great and small. At the end of the fifteenth century a new disease, or perhaps a new form of an old one, syphilis, appeared in Europe and made its way to England, where for about a century it existed as a severe and widespread infection. It was described by Andrew Boorde in his *Breviary of Helthe* in 1547 and more fully by the surgeon William Clowes in 1579 as

> the Morbus Gallicus or Morbus Neapolitanus; but more properly Lues Venera, that is the pestilent infection of filthy lust and termed for the most part in English the French Pocks, a sickness very lothsome, odious, troublesome and dangerous, which spreadeth itself throughout all England and overfloweth as I thinke the whole world.[17]

The problem of finding a name for this sexually transmitted infection had existed since its first appearance in Europe in 1494, brought back, so it was thought, from the New World by Columbus's sailors. A major epidemic occurred at Naples in 1497, following the invasion of Italy by the armies of Charles VIII of France, and it was then taken home by the returning French soldiers: hence the adjectives Neapolitan, Gallic, and French given to the new disease. Its name was eventually settled romantically by the poem *Syphilis sive Morbus Gallicus* (Syphilis or the French Disease) written by the Venetian poet Girolama Fracastoro in 1530, which told how Syphilos, a shepherd boy, offended Apollo, who for a punishment afflicted him with a terrible pox.

The severity of epidemic syphilis in sixteenth-century England excited some graphic and possibly exaggerated comment. According to Clowes,

> It is wonderful to see how huge multitudes there be of such as be infected with it, and that dayley increase, to the danger of the commonwealth, and the stayne of the whole nation: the cause whereof I see none so great as the licentious and beastly disorder of a great number of rogues and vagabonds. The filthy type of many lewd and idell persons, both men and women about the citye of London, and the great number of lewd alehouses, which are the very nests and harbourers of such filthy creatures. . . .[18]

By the end of the century syphilis had been transformed into a somewhat milder, though insidious, disease capable of causing much suffering and sometimes death. In the later eighteenth century Jonas Hanway estimated that 3,000 people a year died in London from venereal diseases. The initial manifestations of syphilis were ulcers or poxes on the skin which tended to heal themselves, and could be treated quite successfully with ointments. But secondary infections sometimes appeared a couple of months later; these might be as severe as smallpox and could lead to disfigurement. Ultimately, by attacking the nervous system, syphilis led to paralysis and insanity. John Aubrey, the irrepressible gossip of the later seventeenth century, reported several scurrilous tragedies. One concerned the Countess of Sussex,

> a great and sad example of the power of Lust and

c

Slavery of it. She was as great a beautie as any in England, and had a good Witt. After her Lord's death (he was jealous) she sends for one (formerly her Footman) and makes him groom of the chamber. He had the Pox and she knew it; a damnable Sott. He was not very handsom, but his body of an exquisite shape. . . . His Nostrils were stufft and borne out with corkes in which were quills to breathe through. About 1666 this Countesse dyed of the Pox.

The penultimate sentence, in fact, suggests that the Countess's paramour suffered from gonorrhea. Another story concerned Elizabeth Broughton, a high-class courtesan— 'her price was verie deare'—who 'at last . . . grew common and infamous and gott the Pox, of which she died'.[19]

Syphilis took its place beside a much older venereal infection, gonorrhea, 'as much an associate of the human race as . . . decay of the teeth'. It was a less dangerous disease than syphilis, but could cause severe pain. In 1590 an unfortunate man, one Enoch Greve from Essex, contracted the complaint and 'drowned himself, being so burned he could not abide the pains'.[20] Gonorrhea also disfigured. According to Aubrey, Sir William Davenant, the dramatist, 'gott a terrible clap of a Black handsome wench that lay in Axe-yard Westminster . . . which cost him his nose, with which unlucky mischance many witts were too cruelly bold'.[21]

If syphilis was a new disease which became less severe in the seventeenth century, smallpox was an old one that became more dangerous. The early history of smallpox in England is obscure. There is no reason to think it was absent in medieval times, but it is not clearly distinguishable. Its presence in the sixteenth century is well known, and Queen Elizabeth was among its more illustrious sufferers. But it was in the seventeenth century that smallpox became evident as a major disease, highly infectious, frequently fatal, and periodically erupting into great epidemics. 'The Small-Pox is usually in all great Towns,' wrote Aubrey, and drawing on his own experience of the west of England, he continued: 'It is observed at Taunton in Somersetshire, and at Sherburne in Dorsetshire, that at the one of them every Seventh Year, and at the other every Ninth Year comes a Small-pox, which the Physitians cannot master.'[22] It caused alarm wherever it appeared. If possible, the dead were quickly buried, and the healthy stayed well clear of any source of infection. 'God knows we have been sequestered from many of our friends' company, who come not near us for fear of infection, and indeed we are very circumspect, careful, and unwilling that any should come to us to impair their health,' wrote a member of a household affected by smallpox in 1628.[23] A century later Daniel Eaton wrote to his master, the Earl of Cardigan, that 'the smallpox are so very much at Uppingham that we durst not send hither for cloth'.[24]

Because smallpox was so infectious and its case mortality so high, it was obviously sensible to avoid contact with it if possible. But it was not a disease that could be avoided like the plague simply by running away from it, and the upper classes were as prone to get it as the poor—in contrast to plague and typhus, which tended to be the prerogative of the lower ranks of society. In 1660 a brother and sister of the newly restored Charles II caught smallpox and died, as did a son of James II. Its most distinguished fatality was Queen Mary, who died in December 1694. Somewhat lower down the social scale, three children of the third Earl of Cardigan had smallpox in 1727, but recovered. Recovery carried with it the risk of scarred complexions. 'Are not these thy steps I trace, In the pure snow of her face?' asked the poet Spilman in 1602, in his poem 'Upon his Lady's Sickness of the Small Pocks'. According to Samuel Pepys, the Duchess of Richmond, mistress of Charles II, was 'of a noble person as ever I did see, but her face worse than it was considerably by the smallpox'. Among the men, Sir John Denham, a seventeenth-century architect, 'was unpolished with the smallpox: otherwise a fine complexion'.[25]

The contribution of smallpox to total mortality in pre-industrial England varied from place to place and time to time. In the major centres of population where the disease was present most of the time, large numbers of people developed an immunity following mild attacks. On the other hand, an outbreak in a rural region, or in a town after several years during which smallpox had been absent, could be attended by a high death rate. The second half of the seventeenth century was punctuated by a number of severe epidemics in England, and, after a lull in the early eighteenth century, the disease returned with full force in 1710 and 1714. During the eighteenth century smallpox became practically endemic in England. In the years 1721–60 it caused ten per cent of all deaths in London, according to the Bills of Mortality, although the true figure may have been higher. Among people actually contracting smallpox fatality rates ranged from 16 to 97 per cent, the highest rates occurring among isolated communities that had no opportunity for building up a natural immunity provided by repeated infections. In the late eighteenth century, however, the severity of smallpox abated, possibly because of a spontaneous change in the nature of the disease and partly as a result of the effects of inoculation and vaccination.

This inventory of illness does not exhaust all the ailments that contributed to the 'incessant Mortality of Mankind'[26] and made life wretched and uncomfortable for the survivors. But it does include some of the commonest epidemics, including the most lethal. Plague, typhus, influenza with pneumonia, alimentary infections and smallpox, were, with tuberculosis, the most dangerous hazards to life. Surveying them, a number of general points can be made. Firstly, they have all ceased to be major causes of death in England, and some of them ceased to be very important even before the nineteenth century. But they had been able to take a grip on pre-industrial communities because of widespread poverty and ignorance. The industrial society created in the nine-teenth century produced no new diseases of its own, except for the importation of Asiatic cholera, and perhaps typhoid fevers in place of typhus.

Secondly, the incidence of specific diseases varied over time. One or two, like infantile diarrhoea, were seasonal, occurring as epidemics practically every summer. Others, such as typhus, were associated particularly with winter and bad harvests. Some epidemics, such as influenza and—as we shall see later—plague, came and went according to no clear-cut rhythm. Taking a long view, some diseases waxed and waned over the years. For example, syphilis was a dangerous epidemic in the sixteenth century but a relatively mild one in the seventeenth; plague was more active between the mid-sixteenth and mid-seventeenth centuries than it had been earlier, and it completely dis-appeared in the third quarter of the seventeenth century; smallpox appears to have been a more serious complaint in the seventeenth than in the sixteenth century. The waning of smallpox by 1800 was possibly partly due to medical advances; but medicine played no part in the decline of dysentery at the end of the eighteenth century. This ebbing and flowing of disease did not escape the notice of contemporaries. Writing some time before 1682, Sir Thomas Browne, the physician and theologian, com-mented:

Certain it is, that the Rickets encreaseth among us; the Small-pox grows more pernicous than the Great: the King's Purse knows that the King's Evil [a tubercular infection] grows more common. Quartan Agues are become no Stranger in Ireland; more common and mortal in England: and though the Ancients gave that Disease very good words, yet now that Bell makes no strange sound which rings out for the Effects thereof....

Some will allow no Diseases to be new, others think that many old ones ceased; and that such which are esteemed new, will have but their time: However the Mercy of God hath scattered the great heap of Diseases, and not loaded any one Country with all: some may be new in one Country which may be old in another.[27]

When Browne wrote the tide of epidemic was running strongly over England bringing about the high mortality and short life-spans of the age.

Finally, variations in the severity of epidemic diseases were not closely related to times of scarcity or times of plenty. True, typhus, in its guise of famine fever, turned up when food was in short supply, but it could be found in years of plenty as well. Dysentery, tuberculosis and the deficiency diseases were all associated with the quality and quantity of food supplies; and practically all ailments took a heavier toll of an ill-nourished population than a well-nourished one. But plague, influenza and smallpox came and went with scant regard for the condition of the harvests. The incidence of dysentery and diarrhoea were determined more by temperature and the congestion of the towns than by the abundance or scarcity of the food supply, while syphilis was the hazard of satisfying the pangs of lust rather than the pangs of hunger. Those Malthusian checks to the growth of population, dearth and disease, were not, in fact, two blades of a pair of scissors operating together, but separate scythes, both of which gathered in the harvest of death. The rhythms of epidemic diseases were frequently obscure, determined by mysterious epidemiological causes that had nothing to do with economic or social conditions. But their consequences had as much, perhaps more, effect on the life of man than sporadic failures of the food supply. Before the nineteenth century they were a major reason why the population increased so slowly.

# 4

## The Ravages of *Rattus Rattus*

PLAGUE was the prince of pestilences. It was not quite the universal predator that some historians have portrayed, and it is doubtful whether it was responsible for all the casualties with which it has been credited. Nevertheless, the spectacular character of its epidemics, its loathsome manifestations and the high death rate it caused among its victims have earned for plague an enviable notoriety. The very word plague, meaning originally a blow—a reference to the violence with which it hit societies—has come to be used for almost any visitation of epidemic disease; and its other descriptions, such as Black Death and Great Pestilence, testify to its dramatic influence.

Plague is a disease of rodents which, in certain conditions, can be transmitted to human beings. There are three forms—bubonic, pneumonic, and septicaemic—the most common of which is bubonic. On the first or second day of infection the patient develops a bubo or swelling of the lymphatic glands in the groin, armpit or neck, accompanied by a high temperature and followed by coma, inflammation of the kidneys, internal bleeding and heart failure. Death occurs in about five days for between 60 and 85 per cent of sufferers, although a patient who survives the bursting of the buboes has some hope of recovery. In some circumstances the disease attacks the lungs, causing the highly infectious and dangerous pneumonic variant of plague; in this form almost certain death occurs within about three days. Even more rapid is the rare septicaemic plague, where general blood-poisoning carries a man from robust health to certain death within twenty-four hours, so quickly, indeed, that the patient displays no other symptoms of the disease.

An epidemic of bubonic plague among humans requires very specific conditions for it to occur, since bubonic plague, unlike the rarer pneumonic and septicaemic forms, is not a very infectious disease. Plague is caused by an internal parasite of rodents, *pasteurella pestis*, a bacterium that multiplies rapidly in the bloodstream of infected animals. All rodents are liable to the disease, but rats, because they often live close to human beings, have been historically the most important in introducing plague to mankind. Both groups of rats, the house or black rat (*rattus rattus*) and the field or brown rat (*rattus norvegicus*) carry the plague; but the major part in English outbreaks has been played by *rattus rattus*. Not only is the brown rat a shyer creature than its black brother, but it was scarcely known in England before about 1730.

The agent responsible for transmitting plague from rats to man is the rat flea (*xenopsylla cheopis*). When a flea feeds on the blood of an infected rat its oesophagus becomes so clogged with rapidly multiplying bacteria that it can no longer ingest its meal. It therefore becomes very hungry. When its rat host dies of plague and chills, the hungry flea looks for fresh pastures, moving to other rats or other animals, including humans. A rat flea does not readily take to humans, preferring its natural hosts, but during a plague epidemic among rodents there may be a shortage of live rats, leaving *xenopsylla cheopis* with little choice but *homo sapiens*. When it bites its new host the clogged flea regurgitates the blood it cannot swallow and in the process introduces the plague bacteria into the bloodstream of its unfortunate victim, who thus contracts plague. However, the bacteria do not normally multiply quickly enough in the human bloodstream to infect the human flea—this is not true of septicaemic plague—so infection is rarely passed directly from man to man. Instead it spreads from rat to flea to man. However, a rat flea can survive for up to six weeks in rags or cloth until another host presents itself, and it is therefore possible for plague to spread from one community to another along trade routes. The flea needs warmth, however, ideally 20–25°C, otherwise it cannot survive. Bubonic plague is therefore primarily a summer disease, dying down in cold weather. In its pneumonic form plague passes from person to person by means of infected droplets coughed from the lungs into the air. It is thus very infectious and, unlike bubonic plague, is not affected by temperature.

The requirements for plague—a population of infected rats living in cosy proximity to a crowd of human beings in warm summer weather—makes it possible to recognise outbreaks of plague more easily than some other diseases. These specific conditions also mean that plague does not normally affect the whole country. After the initial epidemic of the Black Death in the fourteenth century, plague in England became principally a disease of the urban poor who lived in overcrowded cities, in houses built of wood, plaster and straw—desirable residences for rats. The disease sometimes spilled over into better-off districts or travelled into country areas as hungry fleas hitched lifts in bales of cloth or grain sacks. But it was only when bubonic and pneumonic plague existed together that it became a devastating, national calamity.

Three great pandemics of plague have been known to history. The first came to Europe from Asia in the sixth century A.D. and arrived in England in the seventh. The second, the Black Death, swept over Europe in 1348–50 and thereafter erupted intermittently during the next 350 years. The third broke out in India and China at the end of the nineteenth century and still continues, though it has hardly touched Europe.

Although outside the chronological limits of this survey,

no account of plague can leave out the Black Death, for it was the origin of the subsequent epidemics that cropped up in England from time to time until the last great outbreak in London in 1665. In the late 1340s the progress of plague across Europe from Asia Minor was watched with apprehension by Europeans. It reached England in June 1348, entering at the port of Melcombe Regis in Dorset. Ships taking part in the siege of Calais used the port, and it is likely that infected rats disembarked, carrying plague into the community. From this bridgehead plague travelled through the south-west as rats and fleas journeyed along the trade routes and in coastal shipping. Plague also turned east, and by the spring of 1349 had penetrated the whole of southern England and the Midlands. London had an initial visitation in the autumn of 1348, but the major onslaught came in the spring of the following year. During the succeeding months possibly as many as 20,000 or 30,000 died out of a total metropolitan population that could not have exceeded 70,000. Meanwhile plague journeyed northwards and eventually reached the kingdom of Scotland.

Three features of the Black Death stand out: its long period of virulence, its mortality, and its long-term consequences. The Black Death in England ranged over a period of two years, unlike subsequent outbreaks that started in the summer and faded away with the onset of cold weather. This suggests that the pneumonic form of the disease was widespread, keeping the infection active through the winter and helping it to spread rapidly throughout the country. When plague was in France in 1348 it was described by a physician at Avignon:

The said mortality began with us in the month of January and lasted for the space of seven months. It was of two sorts: the first lasted two months, with continuous fevers and expectoration of blood; and men died of it in three days. The second lasted the remainder of the time, also with continuous fever and with external carbuncles and buboes, chiefly in the armpits or the groin, and men died of it in five days.[1]

This was clearly pneumonic plague followed by bubonic. The infection probably ran a particularly widespread course in the 1340s because it was a new disease against which the population possessed no natural immunity. Perhaps this was also the reason for the high rate of mortality. Panic-stricken contemporaries sometimes wrote as though practically the entire population was wiped out by the Black Death, and gullible historians have sometimes taken them at their word. Since the size of the population before the Black Death in England is not known with certainty, it is difficult to judge how many died, or what proportion of all deaths in the years 1348–50 were caused by plague and what by other ailments. The best evidence comes from ecclesiastical sources recording how many clerical appointments became vacant and required filling by new men. The figures varied from about 39 per cent to 49 per cent in different dioceses. Not all vacancies arose from plague: some priests died of old age or other diseases; some resigned or left their posts. Perhaps no more than one-third were plague victims. Fragmentary evidence from secular sources suggests that in some communities mortality was as low as 20 or 25 per cent. The most recent historian of plague has estimated mortality during the Black Death at an even lower figure—no more than about five per cent for England as a whole. But this conclusion can be reached only by denying that pneumonic plague was part of the Black Death, and by attributing, on very insubstantial evidence, many plague deaths to typhus or other infections. There is no reason for expecting plague mortality to have been identical in all communities, and a range from one-fifth to one-third seems reasonable. Although lower than some of the more extreme figures sometimes suggested, no later epidemic of plague ever caused such high mortality over so wide an area.

The immediate reaction to the devastation of the plague was panic. In some districts men and women fled in an attempt to escape infection. On the continent there were uprisings against the Jews, who were held to be somehow responsible. The loss of so many priests, and their replacement by men of less experience, education or spirituality, has been suggested as a cause of the moral decline experienced by the Church during the fifteenth century.

More tangibly, the balance between the supply of men and the supply of land changed. Until the early fourteenth century the population of Europe had been growing: people were becoming plentiful and land correspondingly scarce; wages were falling and rents rising. After the Black Death recurring outbreaks of plague and other epidemics prevented the population from increasing again for over a century. Landlords now found it difficult to get tenants for their farms or labour to work their demesnes, and they largely abandoned the direct cultivation of their estates by the employment of servile labour under the system whereby feudal tenants occupied farms in return for working for the lord of the manor for a certain number of days a week. By 1500 labour services were practically nothing but a memory. Because of the shortage of labour some arable land reverted to pasture and was used for, among other things, the production of wool: the export of fine wool and woollen cloth became one of the mainstays of the English economy. The price of wage labour rose, and cloth manufacturers moved out of the towns into parts of Wiltshire, Gloucestershire and East Anglia, where rural labour was relatively cheap. For many of the poorer members of society the standard of living rose until about 1500, when the renewed growth of population pushed it down once again for the next century and a half.

Following the Black Death, plague remained endemic

in England. On several occasions it flared up to epidemic proportions, but never again on the scale of 1348–50. Between 1350 and 1485 there were about thirty plague years in England: in a dozen of them the epidemics were nationwide, but eight of the outbreaks affected London alone. The most severe epidemic was that of 1361–62, when both bubonic and pneumonic plague occurred together and many of the replacement population born since 1350 died. Another three, perhaps four, national epidemics broke out during the next half century, but increasingly plague became a disease of urban communities. Much the same pattern was repeated in Tudor England. London was the seat of a severe infection in 1500, when between a fifth and a quarter of its inhabitants died. Throughout the first half of the sixteenth century reports of plague in London are frequent, and from 1532 the weekly Bills of Mortality distinguished between deaths from plague and other causes. There were also outbreaks of plague reported from the provinces, although because of the imprecise way in which the word was used by contemporaries it is not always possible to be sure whether it really was plague or some other infection that was meant. On the whole, plague does not seem to have been a major cause of mortality in England during the first half of the sixteenth century.

During the century or so between 1563 and 1665 London suffered five major epidemics of plague as well as several lesser attacks; and there were not many years when the capital was completely free of the disease. The phrase 'great plague' is generally used today to describe the epidemic of 1665, but contemporaries commonly described the most recent outbreak as the 'great plague'. The label has stuck to 1665 only because it proved to be the last of the sequence. But if we were to judge the greatness of a plague epidemic in terms of mortality rates, then the epidemic of 1563 was probably the greatest of them all. According to John Stow, the contemporary historian of London, more than 20,000 people died in the city and its suburbs. Depending on what estimates of metropolitan population one accepts, this represents a death rate of between 22 and 26 per cent—just a little greater than the mortality of 1500. Deaths in London during 1563 were approximately seven times higher than the numbers occurring in non-plague years. This compares with a sixfold increase over average annual non-plague deaths in two later epidemic years, 1603 and 1625, and a fivefold increase in 1665 during the most famous of all the great plagues. Admittedly more people died of plague in 1665 than in 1563, but in the meantime the population of the metropolis had grown six and a half times, so the rate of mortality was a little lower in the later year.

In 1563 plague appeared as early as March: in that month a burial at St Michael's, Cornhill, was described as 'the beginning of the plague in this parish'.[2] But the epidemic did not really get under way until the warm months of June and July. By the end of July plague deaths in the parishes covered by the Bills of Mortality were running at about 300 a week. They rose steeply during August to reach nearly 1,000 a week, and even more steeply in September to 1,600. After a slight lull at the end of the month, the peak of 1,800 deaths was reached in the first week of October. As colder weather set in the epidemic petered out, permitting the Bishop of London in January 1564 to compose 'a short fourme of thankes-gevying to God for ceassing of the contagious sickness of the plague to be used in Common Prayer . . . in the Citie of London, and the rest of his diocese'.[3]

Although God was credited with ending the plague, contemporaries were not unanimous about its origins. The most popular explanation was that it had been introduced into London by soldiers returning home from the besieged and plague-ridden city of Le Havre, where, it was claimed, bubonic plague had been responsible for more deaths than the enemy. But plague was already in

London before the soldiers came home. Possibly a particularly virulent strain of the disease came off one of the merchant ships using the port of London. It is, however, more likely that the epidemic was home-grown but made especially severe by a hot summer and the wretchedly congested conditions of the poorest parishes of London that suffered most during the outbreak.

It is difficult at this distance in time to comprehend the death of a quarter of the population of a large city within the space of five months. On average, every household in London lost one or more of its members during the summer of 1563. Occasionally whole familes were wiped out; for example, an entire family of six died in the parish of St Mary's, Aldermanbury. Most of the victims were the poor of the city, but the better off succumbed as well. Dr John Fryer died in October, followed by his wife and several of his children, all of plague. The city streets echoed to the 'daily jangling and ringing of the bells, the coming of the minister to every house in ministering the communion, the reading of the homily of death, the digging up of graves, the sparring of windows'. Those who could fled from the capital, and the roads leading from the city were blocked with 'waggones, cartes, and horses full laden with yong barnes, for fear of the blacke Pestilence, with them boxes of medicens and sweete perfumes. O God! how fast did they run by hundredes, and were afraid of eche other for feare of smityng.'[4] The Court retreated to Windsor and a ban was placed on trade between Windsor and London. More important, the vital cloth trade between London and the Low Countries was halted in a vain attempt to stop the epidemic; the ban was still in operation in February of the following year, when the governor of the Company of Merchant Adventurers, which handled most of the trade, wrote to the Privy Council asking for it to be lifted since the plague had abated.

Severe though the loss of life was, the city quickly

recovered. Within two years London had made good its loss of population. Indeed, not only after the epidemic of 1563, but also following the other major outbreaks over the next century, the gaps in the ranks were quickly filled by migrants from the provinces; and the population of the metropolis increased throughout the sixteenth and seventeenth centuries despite the periodic setbacks of plague. This remarkable resilience tells us something about the conditions of living in pre-industrial England outside London. For many the contagion-ridden capital offered greater chance of employment than the poverty-ridden countryside. The influx into London in post-plague years was to fill dead men's shoes. Mortality from plague was particularly high among the poor, who supplied much of the casual labour required by the metropolitan economy. There were thus jobs to be had after an epidemic. There was a shortage of people to hold horses, run messages, push carts, carry bundles, heave cargoes at the wharves, deliver letters, sweep steps, and perform the countless tasks demanded in a labour-intensive economy. In addition, as the disease retreated, lawyers—members of one of the most labour-intensive occupations in any age—returned to Westminster, the Court, together with its hangers-on, came back to the capital, merchants resumed their businesses in the city and the country gentry reopened their town houses. But more important were the jobs which were created by the demands of these people and which continuously syphoned off the surplus population of the Home Counties.

The London epidemic of 1563 did not quite become a national outbreak, but it did become sufficiently widespread by August for the Queen to order the Archbishops of Canterbury and York to appoint a day of general prayer and fasting throughout the country for deliverance from the disease. The year 1563 was one of the few years in the sixteenth century when it looked as though plague might spread from its urban strongholds and grip the whole country. Coming as it did after a decade of scarcity, typhus and virulent influenza, its effect was to ease the pressure of population on food supplies, and even to create temporarily the manifestations of a labour shortage. Food prices actually fell for a few years, reversing the long-term upward trend, and wages rose, leading to complaints among employers of the rising cost of labour. However, there was no major demographic crisis, and population in both London and the provinces soon resumed its upward course.

After 1563 London was free of plague for three years. But there were some plague deaths in the city in most years of the later sixteenth century, and in two years, 1578 and 1582, there were moderately severe epidemics of plague, causing between 6,000 and 7,000 deaths on each occasion. This level of mortality was low compared with the mortality of the 'great plagues', but it may be put into perspective by comparing it with the fatality rate of the twentieth-century affliction, road accidents, which in the whole of Great Britain currently kills about 7,500 a year out of a total population exceeding 50 million. London was free of epidemic plague during the later 1580s and early 1590s until 1593, when it was hit by another great epidemic. This time at least 18,000 people perished in the inner parishes alone, and the mortality rate jumped to more than four times its normal level.

This particular epidemic was heralded by an outbreak in the autumn of the previous year, but it died down during the winter, only to erupt again in the spring. By June it was following a familiar course, with plague deaths increasing every week, especially in the densely populated parishes in the east of the metropolis. As the disease spread, so the business of the city came to a halt. The fairs and markets in London and the nearby market towns, on which the capital depended for its supplies of food, were disrupted, and the annual Stourbridge fair, near Cambridge, which was normally attended by tradesmen from London and from all over the country, was cancelled. Within the city itself the authorities did what they could to stem the infection by reissuing old orders for keeping the streets and water supplies clean. In an effort to stop people leaving infected houses crosses were painted on the doors. However, the crosses were 'wiped away in a short space of painting on the doors'; so the Privy Council ordered the city aldermen to take sterner measures and 'cause red crosses to be nayled fast upon the dores of those whose houses are infected and some watch appointed to look unto them that they do not abrode'. Those citizens who could moved to the country, but some stayed to attend to their business or property, trusting in God for protection, like the rector of St Peter's, Cornhill, who wrote in his parish register:

> In a thousand five hundred and ninety-three
> The Lord preserved my house and mee,
> When of the pestilence theare died,
> Full manie a thousand else beside.[5]

Through prayer and prophylactic, or more likely through the coming of cold weather, the epidemic was well on the way to ending by September, though it lingered on through the autumn and a few cases occurred in the following year. Thereafter London was almost free of plague for the rest of the century.

The rest of England was less fortunate. Several provincial towns were touched by plague in 1593, and it was reported from various places, especially in the north of England, for the rest of the decade. In some of these reports the word plague was fairly obviously being used to mean disease in general rather than plague in particular. For example, mortality rates were unusually high in many parishes in the north-west in 1596–97, but the seasonal pattern of deaths suggests not plague but starvation. On the other hand, high mortality in Penrith, Kendal and Carlisle during the summer and autumn of 1598 was certainly caused by bubonic plague. In the period from July to September the monthly mortality in Penrith exceeded a hundred, which was ten to twelve times higher than normal. In all, nearly six hundred people died in Penrith during 1598, the majority of them from plague. This number must have been between one-quarter and one-third of the total population, and was a higher mortality rate than occurred in London in 1593. In a little town like Penrith the population had less chance of building up a resistance to plague than in London, where the disease was endemic.

The reigns of the first two Stuart kings were both inaugurated by serious epidemics of plague in London, and the reign of the third was punctuated by the most notorious of all the great plagues. The epidemics of 1603, 1625, and 1665 between them caused the deaths of between 150,000 and 200,000 men, women and children. There were also two lesser epidemics in 1609 and 1636. In all, between 1603 and 1665 there were nineteen years in which annual plague deaths in London exceeded a thousand and only three years in which plague was completely absent from the city. However, there were also two long periods, one between 1612 and 1624, and the other between 1649 and 1664, when London was free from epidemic plague and suffered only a small number of plague deaths each year. Both these periods ended in a major outbreak that may have been the result of the disease striking a population lacking an immunity built up by earlier infections. During these first seven decades of the seventeenth century plague also erupted from time to time in many provincial towns. But it remained an urban disease and did not become the national scourge in the manner of the Black Death. Finally it disappeared in the 1660s as mysteriously as it had arrived three centuries earlier.

According to the Bills of Mortality, the epidemic of 1603 killed at least 30,000 Londoners. The true figure was certainly higher. It was difficult for the compilers of the Bills of Mortality to keep an accurate count when so many died; and some plague deaths were deliberately suppressed by the unfortunate relatives who feared they would be caught up in quarantine measures if they revealed the true cause of death. The attack started early during an unusually warm May and increased rapidly in intensity during June and July. The peak was reached in early September with over 3,000 deaths a week recorded. Weekly deaths continued at over 2,000 until the end of the month, but the disease was waning visibly by the third week of October and was completely finished by the arrival of the cold December weather. In addition to the dead, the metropolis lost thousands of its population through flight into the countryside. Once again trade was disrupted and markets were cancelled. And James I, who had arrived in his plague-ridden capital from Scotland in May, had his coronation postponed to a more propitious occasion.

The plague followed its normal geographical pattern. It started in the thickly populated parishes in the east of the city and advanced westwards, taking its heaviest toll in the poorest areas. In the words of Thomas Dekker, the London playwright and poet, in *The Wonderful Year*,

Death . . . hath pitcht his tents (being nothing but a heape of winding sheetes tackt together) in the sinfully-polluted Suburbes: the Plague is Muster-Maister and Marshall of the field: Burning Fevers, Boyles, Blaines, and Carbuncles, the Leaders, Lieutenants, Serjeants, and Corporalls: the maine Army consisting . . . of a mingle-mangle, *viz.* dumpish Mourners, merry Sextons, hungry Coffin-sellers, scrubbing Bearers, and nastie Grave-makers: but indeed they are the Pioneers of the Campe, that are employed onely (like Moles) in casting up of earth and digging of trenches; Feare and Trembling (the two Catch-polles of Death) arrest every one:

No parley will be granted, no composition stood upon,
But the Allarum is strucke up, the *Toxin* ringes out for
life, and no voice is heard but *Tue, Tue, Kill, Kill*; the
little Belles onely . . . do yet goe off, and make no great
worke for wormes, a hundred or two lost in every skirm-
ish . . . yet by these desperat sallies, what by the open
setting upon them by day, and secret Ambuscadoes by
night, the skirts of *London* were pittifully pared off, by
little and little.[6]

Those who could retreated before the advance of death,
'some riding, some on foote; some without bootes, some in
their slippers; by water, by land; in shoales swam they
westwards'. So great was the demand for transport that
'Hacknies, water-men and Wagons were not so terribly
imployed many a yeare'.

In the beleaugered city, Dekker described scenes of
desolation. Plague, advancing like a conqueror, 'plaide
the tyrant':

Men, women & children dropt downe before him:
houses were rifled, streetes ransackt, beautiful maydens
throwne on their beddes, and ravisht by sicknes, rich-
mens Cofers broken open, and shared amongst prodigall
heires and unthriftie servants, poore men used poorely,
but not pittifully. . . .

The streets echoed with

the loude groanes of raving sicke men, the strugling
panges of soules departing: in every house griefe
striking up an Allarum; Servants crying for maisters,
wives for husbands, parents for children, children for
their mothers. . . .

Pits were dug at night for the dead, and at dawn

A hundred hungry graves stand gaping, and every one
of them (as at a breakfast) hath swallowed downe ten
or eleven liveless carcases: before dinner, in the same

gulfe are twice so many more devoured: and before the sun takes his rest, those numbers are doubled. Three-score that not many hours before, had every one severall lodgings very delicately furnisht, are now thrust altogether into one close roome: a little noisom roome, not fully ten foote square.

Dekker also noted that, far from promoting Christian virtues of love and charity, plague did the reverse. Country people eyed refugees from London with suspicion and 'wisht rather they had falne into the hands of Spaniards'. 'Hearbe-wives and Gardeners' cashed in on the disaster, 'for the prices of flowers, hearbes, and garlands, rose wonderfully in so much that Rosemary which had wont to be sold for 12. pence an armefull, went now for sixe shillings a handfull'. In the city sextons, who controlled the parish graveyards, 'now had better doings than either Tavernes or bawdy-houses'.

Dekker was perhaps not a clinically precise observer, but his graphic descriptions manage to convey the horror of plague and the fear it created. London to Dekker appeared 'forsaken like a Lover, forlorne like a widow, and 'disarmde of all comfort'. No other malady created such consternation. True, plague could be avoided by evacuation and by reasonable attention to household and personal cleanliness; some contemporaries realised that the disease attacked chiefly 'such as do not generally regard clean and sweet keeping, and where many are pestered together in alleys and houses'.[7] Yet even the wealthy found it difficult to avoid dirt and congestion in London, and it was all too easy to become the unwitting host for an infected flea. Thus plague impressed Dekker and other contemporary observers as an unpredictable and terrifying enemy which caused more havoc to economic and social arrangements than any other malady. Even when the epidemic was over and the refugees had returned, trade revived, and fresh migrants taken the place of the deceased, there remained 'the ghosts of those more (by many) than 40,000 that by the virulent poison of infection have bin driven out of [their] earthlie dwellings' to remind the survivors of what the next visitation would be like.

After the epidemic of 1603, plague occurred in London in every year until 1611, although there were only a small number of cases each year, except in 1609 when there was a considerable outbreak. Then came a long period during which bubonic plague became an insignificant cause of death in London. The chronology was similar in the provinces. In 1603 plague spread from London into the Home Counties, not surprisingly in view of the large number of Londoners who had retreated to the countryside, and several provincial towns experienced epidemics of their own. Plague also cropped up in various places during the summer of virtually every year until 1610, but then, as in London, it petered out until the next great epidemic in 1625.

The coincidence, both in 1603 and 1625, of a new king with a new epidemic of plague was not lost on contemporaries, who offered two somewhat contradictory explanations for the phenomenon. According to one view, God was purging a sinful nation—or at least its capital—of its wickedness in readiness for the new ruler to assume his responsibilities. According to the other, loyal and sturdy Englishmen were carried off to the kingdom of heaven to keep the deceased monarch company:

> So mighty *James* (the world's admired mirour)
> *True faiths defending friend*, sterne Foe to Errour,
> When he Great Britaines Glorious Crowne did leave,
> A Crowne of endless glory to receive,
> Then presently in less than eight months space
> Full eighty thousand followed him apace.

These unctuous lines, of much rhyme but little scansion, were written by John Taylor, the 'Water Poet',[8] a Thames bargeman turned versifier, who, in his way, provided as wordy a description of the plague of 1625 as Thomas Dekker gave of the epidemic two decades earlier.

This fresh epidemic caused between 40,000 and 50,000 deaths in the metropolitan region, out of a total population of just under 300,000. In terms of mortality rates, therefore, the plague of 1625 was less severe than the outbreaks of both 1563 and 1603, but worse than the epidemic of 1665. The chronology of contagion followed familiar lines:

A Healthful *April*, a diseased *June*,
And dangerous *July*, brings all out of tune.

The plague built up during May, which was warm, and increased rapidly to reach a peak of over 4,000 deaths a week in August. It subsided rapidly during September and October and came to an end in November with the arrival of 'frostie and kindlie weather which it may please God to send'. No metropolitan parish escaped, but the infection was worst in the densely populated area just to the east of the city proper, where over eighty per cent of all the deaths occurring during the summer months were caused by plague.

The economic and social consequences were similar to those of earlier years. The Court retreated to the countryside and once more a Stuart king had his coronation postponed because of plague. Markets and fairs were cancelled, shops shut up, and trade came to a halt.

Streets thinly man'd [wrote Taylor] with wretches every day,
Which have no power to flee, or meanes to stay.
In some whole street (perhaps) a shop or twaine
Standes open, for small takings, and lesse gaine,
And every closed window, door, and stall,
Makes each day seeme a solemne Festivall.

The only business to flourish was that of death:

All Trades are dead, or almost out of breath,
But such as live by sicknesse or by death;
The Mercers, Grocers, Silk-men, Goldsmiths, Drapers,
Are out of Season, like noone-burning Tapers:
All functions faile, almost, through want of buyers,
And every Art and Mystery turne *Dyers*.

By contrast, coffin-makers, sextons, searchers-out of corpses and dog-killers enjoyed booming business during the general depression:

These are *Grave* Trades, that doe get and save,
Whose Gravitie bringes many to their *grave*.

Dog-killers found a market for their services because of a common belief that dogs spread the plague. In 1625 the parish of St Margaret's, Westminster, paid £2 17s. 8d. for 'braining brawling Curs, and foisting hounds', or 1½d. for each of 466 animals.

There was the usual exodus of those able to get away from London, in spite of feeble attempts by the city authorities and the Privy Council to enforce quarantine regulations. But Londoners were unwelcome in the countryside, as Taylor observed:

The name of *London* now bothe farre and neare,
Strikes all the Townes and Villages withe feare;
And to be thought a *Londoner* is worse,
Than one that breakes a horse or takes a purse.

Occasionally Londoners were physically assaulted by frightened countrymen, although more often they were coldly ostracised and physical contact was avoided—like the plague. Those who were compelled to stay behind did what they could to preserve themselves from sickness with the help of doctors and apothecaries, or by more homely means:

One with a piece of tasseld well *tarr'd Rope*,
Doth with that nose-gay keepe himselfe in hope:

Another doth a wisp of wormwood pull,
And with great judgement crams his nostrils full:
A third takes off his socks from's sweating feet,
And makes them his perfume amongst the street. . . .
Whilst *Billets*, Bonefire-like, and *Faggots* drie
Are burnt i' the streetes, the Aire to purifie.

The inhabitants of the Home Counties had some reason
to be suspicious of the refugees pouring from the capital,
for outbreaks of plague became widespread in Essex,
Kent, Middlesex, and elsewhere during 1625. Plague was
also reported from East Anglia and the south-west,
although there is no reason to link these outbreaks with
the London infection, and the epidemic never became
nationwide. London itself stayed fairly free of plague after
1625 until 1631, when there was a small outbreak. Some
provincial centres were more seriously affected. There was
a fairly severe epidemic in London in 1636 which killed
10,000 or more people. The spring and early summer
of that year were cool and the disease was slow to get
going, which perhaps accounts for the comparatively low
mortality of the epidemic in London. But in other parts of
the country plague took a heavy toll. There were outbreaks in East Anglia, the Midlands and the north-east.
The most disastrous was at Newcastle, where 5,000 people
died of plague out of a population of about 18,000
    The late 1630s and the 1640s were generally plague-
ridden years in London; the worst year after 1636 was
1647, which had 3,500 deaths. The provincial towns were
probably even more seriously affected in proportion to
their populations in these decades. Possibly the high level
of troop movements during the 1640s and the overcrowding caused by the billeting of troops in the garrison towns
helped the spread of plague. According to one medical
historian, all the provincial epidemics occurred in towns
that were besieged, or had been besieged, or had been
occupied by bodies of troops or by garrisons. Such an

explanation, however, does not apply to the Devonshire village of Colyton, where 392 people died between November 1645 and October 1646, almost all of them from plague. This represented roughly one-fifth of the population of the village. Unlike London, there was no speedy recovery in subsequent years. On the contrary, the epidemic triggered off a new demographic pattern of high mortality and low fertility that persisted in the village for the rest of the century.

During the 1650s and early 1660s plague was dwindling in England—indeed, it was in retreat throughout Europe. During the sixteen years 1649–64 London was free of anything approaching an epidemic. When plague returned with devastating consequences in 1665 it proved to be the last major visitation known in England. The last European epidemic occurred at Marseilles in 1720—the final twitch of a disease that had scourged Europe since the fourteenth century.

During the 'great plague' of London in 1665 at least 70,000 people perished of bubonic plague; and the figure might have been as high as 100,000 if estimates of the concealed deaths and the mortality of the out-parishes are taken into account. The mortality rate was lower than in any of the earlier major outbreaks except for that of 1593, although the death-toll of between 70,000 and 100,000 in less than half a year was not a figure to be taken lightly. The onset of the disease followed its classical pattern. In early June plague deaths recorded in the Bills of Mortality were less than a hundred a week, but they increased rapidly in June, July and August to reach a peak of over 7,000 deaths a week by September. September was the worst month with more than 26,000 recorded deaths, followed by 14,000 in October. But even before the weather turned really cold, plague was on the decline. At the end of November Pepys wrote in his diary that he had 'great hopes of further decrease because of this day's being a very exceeding hard frost, and continues freezing'.[9] In

December plague deaths dropped to under a hundred for the month.

Reactions to the plague were no different from those that occurred in earlier epidemics. Courtiers, lawyers, politicians, the wealthy, even many doctors and clergy, withdrew to healthier surroundings in the country; and trade came almost to a halt. The situation was described almost sixty years after the event by Daniel Defoe in his semi-fictional *Journal of the Plague Year*,[10] which was based on contemporary accounts:

> All that had friends or estates in the country retired with their families; and when, indeed, one would have thought the very city itself was running out of the gates, and that there would be nobody left behind; you may be sure from that hour all trade, except such as related to immediate subsistence, was, as it were, at a full stop.

The virtue of Defoe's prosaic account over the colourful alliterations of Dekker and the cumbersome stanzas of Taylor was the close analysis it offers of the economic consequences of plague. With the fall in the population of the capital, 'all master-workmen in manufactures, especially such as belonged to ornament and the less necessary parts of the people's dress, clothes, and furniture for houses . . . dismissed their journeymen and workmen, and all their dependants'. The movement of shipping in and out of London came to a virtual halt, creating unemployment among customs officers, watermen, carmen, porters, 'and all the poor whose labour depended upon the merchants'; sailors and those engaged in the provisioning and fitting of ships were all out of employment. Economic contraction went even further as

> All families retrenched their living as much as possible. . . . An innumerable multitude of footmen, serving-men, shopkeepers, journeymen, merchants' bookkeepers, and such sort of people, and especially

poor maid-servants, were turned off, and left friendless
and helpless, without employment and without habita-
tion. . . .

Growing unemployment became a threat to public order
that was alleviated only by charity given out by the Lord
Mayor and aldermen of the city and by the growth of
certain alternative employments directly connected with
the plague itself. These included watchmen to guard over
infected houses. According to Defoe, there were ten thousand such houses, each requiring two watchmen, one by
night and one by day. Then there were nurses for the
sick, men to drive the dead-carts, bearers to clear the
corpses from stricken houses, grave-diggers, and labourers to clear away the cadavers before they 'perished and
rotted in a dreadful manner'. As Defoe explained, 'Had it
not been that the number of poor people who wanted
employment and wanted bread . . . was so great that
necessity drove them to undertake anything and venture
anything, they would never have found people to be
employed.'

One man of substance who remained in London
throughout the plague, although he sent his household to
Woolwich, was Samuel Pepys. He continued about his
business in spite of the epidemic and observed the effect
of mass death upon the capital. The first reference to the
'Sicknesse' appeared in his diary on 30 April, and on 10
June he recorded with a note of alarm that plague was at
the house of 'my good friend and neighbour', Dr Burnet
in Fenchurch Street. At the end of the month Pepys went
to Whitehall where he found the Court preparing to move
out of town, but he consoled himself with the thought that
the business section of the city was still fairly free of
infection compared with the out-parishes. Thereafter
plague was rarely absent from the pages of his diary, as
he travelled fairly freely about the town. On 25 July
he went by coach, 'not meeting one coach going nor

coming from my house thither or back agan, which is very strange'. He was alarmed the following day by a plague death in his own parish, St Olave's, 'so that I begin to think of setting things in order, which I pray God enable me to put, both as to soul and body'. Another anxious moment occurred on 15 August: as Pepys was returning home late at night he 'met a dead corps, of the plague, in the narrow alley, just bringing down a little pair of stairs—but I thank God I was not much disturbed at it. However, I shall beware of being late abroad again.' He also observed the frequent funeral processions still taking place in spite of regulations prohibiting them. Pepys marvelled at 'the madness of people of the town, who will . . . come in crowds along with the dead corps to see them buried'. As the epidemic continued on its way, the Thames became empty of boats and grass could be seen growing in Whitehall. Even in October, when the worst was over and Pepys took a walk to the Tower, he reflected:

> Lord, how empty the streets are, and melancholy, so many poor sick people in the streets, full of sores, and so many sad stories overheard as I walk, everybody talking of their dead, and that man sick, and so many in this place, and so many in that.

By the end of the month, however, he was more cheerful: 'The Change pretty full, and the town begins to be lively again—although the streets very empty and most shops shut.' At the end of November, things were getting back to normal; and 'great joy we have this week', as the weekly Bills of Mortality recorded only 333 plague deaths and Pepys prepared to bring his wife and servants back to London. He had, as he says, much to be thankful for:

> My whole family hath been well all this while, and all my friends I know of, saving my Aunt Bell, who is dead, and some children of my Cousin Sarah's of the plague. But many such as I know, very well, dead. Yet to our

great joy, the town fills apace, and shops begin to open
again. Pray God continues the plague's decrease—for
that keeps the Court away from the place of business,
and so all goes to wrack as to public matters, they at
their distance not thinking of it.[11]

God did continue the plague's decrease. It returned for
a while in 1666 at a level high enough to spread alarm,
but after July, during which there were a couple of hundred plague deaths in London, the disease dwindled right
away. In the Home Counties plague was endemic throughout 1665 and 1666, and it cropped up also in the provinces,
possibly introduced from the main source of infection in
London. The most famous incident of the provincial outbreaks was the calamity that overwhelmed the village of
Eyam in Derbyshire. According to popular account, the
village tailor received a box of old clothes from London
in September 1665, among which were lodged infected
rat fleas, hungry for a meal after their long journey. They
found an unwitting host in the person of the tailor's
servant, who became ill and died of plague within four
days. Five more deaths had occurred by the end of September; there were nineteen in October, and a few in each
of the winter months. The following June the disease
flared into fresh activity, and the summer was made
memorable by the efforts of the rector of the parish, who
tried to prevent his flock from fleeing from the village
and carrying the infection to other parts of the county.
He was apparently successful, although at the cost of the
lives of 259 villagers out of a population of about 350.
Whether, in fact, all the inhabitants obeyed the clerically
imposed quarantine is questionable; the population of the
village quite speedily recovered after 1666, suggesting
that some did leave the village and returned when the
danger was over.

In 1667 there was an outbreak of plague at Nottingham,
which was probably its last occurrence in seventeenth-

century England. The disease then disappeared for two
and a half centuries. There was an outbreak of bubonic
plague in Glasgow in 1900 and another in Liverpool the
following year; while in Suffolk between 1906 and 1918
there were several cases of a disease reputed to be plague.
But these were stray importations of the epidemic then
ravaging Asia. As an English disease, plague may be said to
have come to an end in the 1660s. It was not, however,
obvious at the end of the seventeenth century that plague
had gone, almost for ever. For years after 1665 an outbreak of fever, or some other omen, was held to presage
plague. A mild winter in 1680 caused John Aubrey to
record a piece of gossip: 'Mr Fabian Philips sayes the
winter 1625 before the Plague was such a mild winter as
this.'[12] The great plague at Marseilles in 1720 led many
to think that the disease would come back to England, and
it was the occasion of the publication of Defoe's *Journal
of the Plague Year*, recalling the disaster of 1665.

But plague had gone, and no one knew why. Even today
the reasons are obscure. One explanation may be immediately rejected: the fire of London in 1666. Rats and fleas
certainly perished, but there were plenty left, especially
in the out-parishes unaffected by the blaze where the
disease had always been especially virulent. In any case,
a fire in London would not explain the ending of plague
in the provinces, nor its disappearance from Europe.

Another theory may be also quickly discounted: that
the development of shipping routes to the East broke the
chain of infection. This view assumes that a reservoir of
plague existed in India—it was in origin an Asiatic
disease—which was periodically transmitted to Europe
by infected rats and their fleas as they travelled with the
overland caravans across Asia Minor to the Levantine
ports where they boarded ship for western Europe. Once
trade between Europe and Asia took to the sea route
round the Cape, it is argued, re-infection of Europe became impossible since the fleas of infected rats could not

survive the long sea voyage. In fact, the chronology of
this explanation is wrong: the sea-borne routes to the
East were established long before plague disappeared
from Europe. Neither is it correct to regard plague as a
disease that was regularly re-introduced into Europe from
Asia: from its arrival in the mid-fourteenth century to
its passing at the end of the seventeenth, plague was
endemic in England. The London and provincial epidemics of the sixteenth and seventeenth centuries were
home-grown.

The retreat of plague has been explained by 'an
obscure ecological revolution among rodents'. Plague, it
will be remembered, was a disease of rodents, transmitted
to man by the flea *xenopsylla cheopis*. The constant companion of medieval and early modern man was *rattus
rattus*, the black rat, which 'breeds in human homes and
ships and thrives best on cereals, the chief food of man;
but above all . . . is the favourite host of *xenopsylla
cheopis*, which is the plague flea *par excellence*'.[18] But
'sometime after 1660' the black rat was driven out, or
starved out, by the brown rat, with less liking for human
habitations, and with a flea of its own, *nosopsyllus fas-
ciatus*, that has even less liking for the taste of human
blood than the flea of the black rat. Thus, although brown
rats contracted plague, they were less likely to share it
with humans than black rats. Unfortunately, the neatness
of this explanation is upset by the fact that brown rats
did not effectively colonise England until more than half
a century after plague had ceased to be a tribulation of
the country's human inhabitants.

We are left, therefore, wondering whether rats or men,
or both, developed an immunity to plague in the later
seventeenth century, or whether the disease changed its
nature. There were signs even before the 1660s that plague
was receding in London. Thirty years separated the two
major epidemics of 1563 and 1593 and there were ten
years between the outbreaks of 1593 and 1603; but sub-

D

sequently there were gaps of twenty-two and forty years between major epidemics. True, there were other, lesser outbreaks in intervening years, and practically no year in which London was entirely free from plague. However, the epidemics of 1625 and 1665 were both preceded by long periods during which plague, although present, killed only in dribs and drabs.

Could some kind of immunity have become established in populations regularly exposed to plague? The possibility that this was so is suggested by the heavy toll the disease exacted when it hit small provincial communities, which, unlike London, did not live with plague as a constant companion. But there are difficulties even with this explanation. If familiarity bred immunity, why did bubonic plague strike with such fury in London in 1625 and 1665? And why did the whole English population remain unaffected after the 1660s? If the disease changed its nature, what was the reason? These are problems for epidemiologists rather than historians. To the latter, plague has proved a mystery both in its coming and in its departing. It is only certain that in the late seventeenth century, without any improvement in the material environment in which men lived, and without advances in the knowledge of disease or medicine which men possessed, bubonic plague ceased to be a reason why pre-industrial Englishmen died in such profusion.

# 5

# Quacks, Cures and Cleanliness

AGAINST the onslaughts of death, dearth and disease
were ranged the defences of prayer, medicine and magic,
supplemented by such measures of private and public
hygiene as might be thought possible or appropriate. In
a period when God's hand was seen in all things, prayer
was the universal palliative for all human afflictions, possessing the peculiar quality of being thought efficacious
whether it worked or whether it failed. If the former, and
famine was averted or epidemic conquered, then the
credit was God's who had hearkened to the prayers of his
suffering children. If the latter, the fault lay not in the
prayer but in those who prayed for not yet reaching the
pitch of penitence meriting relief from their miseries.
During periods of disaster in pre-industrial England days
of fasting were frequently proclaimed by governments
and bishops, and prayers were published petitioning the
Almighty to show mercy. During the plague epidemic of
1665 William Lilly, the astrologer, attended a public
service in London:

> The *Sunday* before the great Bill [of Mortality, which
> was published weekly on Tuesdays] came forth, which
> was of 5,000 and odd Hundreds, there was appointed a
> Sacrament at Clement Danes; during the distributing
> thereof I do well remember we sang thirteen Parts of
> the One hundred and nineteenth Psalm. One *Jacob*
> our Minister (for we had three that Day, the Com-
> munion was so great) fell sick as he was giving the

Sacrament, went home, and was buryed of the Plague the *Thursday* following. Mr *James* another of the Ministers fell sick, ere he had quite finished, had the Plague, and was thirteen Weeks ere he recovered. Mr *Whitacre*, the last of the three, escaped not only then, but all the Contagion following without any Sickness at all; though he Officiated at every Funeral, and buryed all manner of People, whether they died of the Plague or not. He was given to drink, seldom could preach more than one quarter of an Hour at a Time.[1]

If Lilly noticed any irony in the sequence of events he chose to ignore it and did not draw the superficial, though erroneous, conclusion that alcohol might provide a better protection from plague than prayer. But in the light of such experiences it was prudent to give the Almighty a helping hand. And 'to whom in an Epidemical confusion of Wounds', asked Dekker, 'should a man flye, but to Phyysicke and Chirurgery?'[2]

To judge the adequacy of the defences offered by the medical profession in pre-industrial England against death and disease we need to decide, first what we mean by the profession—how was it constituted? and who should be numbered among its ranks? We also need to understand something of the nature of their knowledge of the functioning of the body and the causes of illnesses. Finally, we require information about the quality of the treatment that was offered.

A profession may be defined as a body of men and women trained in a specific skill, educated in a specific corpus of knowledge, and organised within an institution which maintains standards and distinguishes between members of the profession and outsiders. In the sixteenth century there were three embryonic groups emerging to form the medical profession: apothecaries, surgeons, and physicians; although in the early part of the century, 'the apothecary was still a variety of grocer, the surgeon still a variety of barber, and the physician but just ceasing to be an ecclesiastic'.[3] Physicians were the most exclusive of the three groups. In the Middle Ages medical science, such as it was, was virtually a branch of theology, and in early Tudor England physicians were often priests, such as Andrew Boorde, who had been a Carthusian monk. By an act of 1511 the power to license physicians who were not university graduates was granted to the bishops, and in London to the Dean of St Paul's. Seven years later, in 1518, the profession formally broke away from ecclesiastical control with the incorporation of the Royal College of Physicians, membership of which was confined to those possessing the degree of Doctor of Medicine from the universities of Oxford or Cambridge. Its first president was Thomas Linacre, a graduate of Padua and Oxford, a learned classical scholar, and tutor and physician to the courts of Henry VII and Henry VIII. Linacre epitomised the physician of his time. The medical faculties at Oxford and Cambridge were semi-moribund in the early sixteenth century, and a training at one of the continental medical schools, such as Padua, was therefore essential; continental degrees were then registered at either Oxford or Cambridge, which accepted them as equivalents of their own degrees. A command of Latin and Greek was essential for the reading of Hippocrates, Galen and other texts on which Tudor medicine was based, and a broad education was also required to help with diagnosis and prescription—and to bolster up the authority of the physician.

The basic educational requirements of the physician were outlined by Andrew Boorde. The very title page of his *Breviary of Helthe* reflected the linguistic bias of Tudor medicine, for the book was described as 'expressynge the obscure termes of Greke, Araby, Latyn, and Barbary, in to englysh'. In the 'prologe', designed to reassure fellow physicians that he was not divulging their trade secrets by rendering medicine into the vernacular, Boorde wrote:

Every phisicion ought to knowe fyrst lernynge and then practyce, that is to saye fyrste to have gramer to understand what he doth rede in latyn. Than to have Logycke to discusse or dyffine by argumentacion the trouth from the falsehood. . . . And then to have a Rethorycke or an eloquent tonge the whyche shulde be placable to the herers of his worde. And also to have Geomatry, to ponder the way the dregges or porcions the whiche ought to be ministred. Arythmetrycke is necessary to be had concerninge numeration but above al thynges next to gramer a phisicion must have surely his Astronomy to knowe howe whan & what tyme evey medecine ought to be ministred. And than fynally to knowe naturall phylosophy, the whych consysteth in the knowledge of natural thyngs. And al these thinges had, than is a man apt to study physicke by speculacion. And speculacion obtayned than boldly a man maye practyse phisicke.[4]

Not surprisingly, the supply of persons with such qualifications was limited, and such physicians as there were tended to practise at Court and among the upper classes; the poor had to make do without their grammar and their astronomy.

The gap created by the scarcity of physicians was partly filled by apothecaries. These were originally dealers in herbs and spices, and were closely associated with the grocers who imported spices and pharmaceutical materials into England. With their knowledge of the medical properties of various plants, apothecaries took to treating patients as well as compounding and supplying medicines prescribed by physicians. They lacked a professional organisation of their own during the sixteenth century, but London apothecaries were members of the Grocers' Company. In 1617, however, after a considerable struggle, the apothecaries broke away from the grocers and received a royal charter establishing the 'Worshipful Society of the Art & Mystery of Apothecaries', which controlled the activities of the profession in and around London. Socially and professionally apothecaries remained inferior to the physicians, and on the completion of their seven-year apprenticeships apothecaries had to submit to examination by the College of Physicians before they could become full members of their own company.

The lowest ranks of the medical hierarchy were occupied by the surgeons, the mechanics of the profession. Surgeons frequently learned their trade while serving with armies, for which they were as necessary as armourers and farriers. From as early as 1462 surgeons in London had been members of the guild of barbers, and a Company of Barber-Surgeons was established in 1540 at the instigation of Thomas Vicary, sergeant-surgeon to Henry VIII. This company became responsible for standards of practice, but licences to practise surgery were granted by the Bishop of London. A separate Company of Surgeons, eventually to become the Royal College of Surgeons, was not established until 1745. The association between barbers and surgeons stemmed from their related functions; it also represented a rationalisation in the use of capital, since the scissors and razors of one craft could be employed in the other. Broadly speaking, surgeons dealt with wounds, fractures and external disorders; internal surgery was almost unknown.

The social inferiority of surgeons compared with physicians was implied in Boorde's description of the qualities needed by a good surgeon. Surgery was indeed a 'laudable science', esteemed for its 'great utility'. But unlike the scholarly requirements of the physician, 'masters of Chierrurgy' ought to have 'good wyttes & memory, evermore to be diligent & tendable about theyr cures'. They should have 'a good eye and a stedfast hande', and 'be wyse, gentyll, sober, and nat dronken, circumspect, and lerned, and to promyse no more than they be able to performe with goddes helpe, and nat to be boystrouse aboute his pacientes but lovyngly to comfort them'.[5] These were the practical virtues of the craftsman (although he could not always be trusted to possess them) rather than the learned attributes of the gentleman. They were gained by apprenticeship and service on the battle-field rather than by reading in the secluded cloisters of continental colleges.

The three-way division between physician, apothecary and surgeon was not rigidly upheld, and by the middle of the seventeenth century it was not unknown for a man to describe himself as 'chirurgeon and apothecary'; indeed, in the early sixteenth century John Caius, a distinguished physician and scholar, had lectured on anatomy both to the College of Physicians and to the Company of Barber-Surgeons. Nevertheless, the aloofness felt by physicians to their lesser brethren persisted and sometimes hardened into downright hostility. The College of Physicians did not allow surgeons to administer medicines, except under directions from a physician, although the college statutes did permit a physician to perform surgical operations. During the seventeenth century the College of Physicians spent a good deal of time chivvying surgeons who had prescribed a pill or two without permission. Not surprisingly, the surgeons sometimes complained. For example, a group of surgeons told the House of Commons in 1621 that the physicians 'do not only take unto themselves the arts of Physition, Chirurgion and Apothecary, but do likewise go aboute to restraine your petitioners from using unto their greved and wounded patients such wound-drinkes, potions, and other inward remedies as they . . . have found necessary for the recovery of their patients'.[6] In 1633 William Harvey, famous for his work on the circulation of the blood, drew up rules for the government of St Batholomew's Hospital in London, where he was physician, that clearly reflected the professional inferiority of surgeons. Among other things, it was ordered

That the chirurgions in all difficult cases, or where inward phisick may be necessary shall consult with the Do<sup>r.</sup> at the tyme he sitteth once in the weeke. . . .

That no chirurgion or his man doe trepan the head, peirce the body, dismember or doe any great operacion on the body of any but with the approbacon & by direction of the Do<sup>r.</sup> . . .

That every churugion shall followe the directions of the Do<sup>r.</sup> in outward operacions for inward causes, for recovery of every patient under their severall cures, & to this end shall once in the weeke attend the Do<sup>r.</sup> . . .

That the Apothecary Matron & Sisters doe attend the Do<sup>r.</sup> when he sitteth to give direction & prescripts, that they may fully conceave his directions & what is to be done. . . .[7]

Whether the social distinctions existing in the medical profession had any effects, good or bad, on its customers is difficult to judge. The exclusiveness of the College of Physicians certainly limited the supply of medical men available. According to one medical historian, there was only one physician for every 23,000 of the population in early Tudor England. The College was particularly restrictive in London. In 1589 it had thirty-eight members for a population of perhaps 100,000; by the 1640s it had much the same number serving a population four times as great. In Norwich, the second city of England with a population of about 13,000 in 1525, there were no physicians, surgeons or apothecaries, but only fifteen barbers. In 1569, when the city was not much bigger, there were thirteen barbers, three surgeons, two apothecaries, but no physicians. The situation gradually improved, however, and in the first forty years of the seventeenth century a total of seventeen doctors practised in Norwich. In a wider context, among a sample of 27,000 wills registered for probate throughout England and Wales during the period 1653–56 there were only 138 medical men, consisting of twenty-seven apothecaries, eighty-two barbers, surgeons and barber-surgeons, and twenty-nine physicians, practitioners of physic, or holders of the degree of MD.

The traditional training of the physician was based on classical Greek and Latin texts. The bulk of Greek medical teaching was available in the voluminous works of Galen, written in the second century A.D. His influence was so great that the term 'Galenist' was commonly applied to orthodox medical men even as late as the seventeenth century. When William Harvey was a student at Cambridge instruction was 'limited to medical readings and disputations on such subjects as pulses, urines, and drugs, Galen's writings, and the *Aphorisms* of Hippocrates'.[8] By the sixteenth century many texts of Galen and other early writers were so corrupt that the Renaissance physician needed a command of Greek and Latin to be able to recover the purity of the originals.

Greek, Roman and Arabic medical traditions had all frowned upon the dissection of human bodies, and much of Galen's anatomical work, therefore, was based upon the dissection of animals, particularly pigs, from which many erroneous inferences were drawn about human anatomy. The physiological system taught in Galenist medicine was that of the four humours—blood (hot and moist), phlegm (cold and moist), yellow bile (hot and dry), and black bile (cold and dry)—which governed the four temperaments—sanguine, phlegmatic, choleric and melancholic. Ill-health was believed to result from the imbalance of the humours, and could be corrected according to the doctrine of contraries: for heat apply cold, for dryness moisture, and so on. The most common diagnostic tool was the inspection of the patient's urine, which was collected in a flask for the purpose. As a method, it was supported by the taking of the pulse and the making of astrological observations—hence the stress on astronomy as part of the training of physicians in the sixteenth century. By the seventeenth century doubts were creeping in about the value of urinoscopy: 'for urine is a strumpet, or an harlot, for it will lye, and the best doctour of physicke of them all maye be deceived in an urine'.[9] The doubtful value of the urine testing gave rise to many bitter jests. For example, John Taylor was contemptuous of physicians with their urine flasks during the London plague of 1625:

Some men their are that rise by others falls,
Propheticke Augurists in urinals,
Those are right Water-men, and rowe so well,
They either land their *Fares* in Heav'n or Hell.
I never knew them yet to make a stay
And land at Purgatorie, by the way:
The reason very plainely doth appeaire,
Their Patients feele their Purgatorie here.[10]

Against virtually every disorder of the human constitution physicians aimed their twin blunderbuss of bleeding and purging. Bleeding was done by cupping, leeching, or the opening of veins; it frequently left the patient utterly debilitated and still in possession of his original complaint. Purging was sometimes done with ferocious vigour and occasionally had fatal consequences. John Aubrey told of an acquaintance

who had a beloved daughter, who had been a long time ill, and received no benefit from her Physitians. She dream'd that a Friend of hers, deceased, told her, that if she gave her Daughter a Drench of Yewgh powdered, she would recover. She gave the drench and it killed her, whereupon she grew almost distracted. Her Chamber Maid to Complement her, and to mitigate her Grief, said surely that could not kill her; she would adventure to take the same herselfe; she did so and died also.[11]

The herb gardens, hedgerows, grocers' shops and waste lands were scoured for products to compound into concoctions intended to supplement the leech and the enema.

In 1575 Lord Burghley, Elizabeth's chief minister, was advised that 'the ouse of Asshen barke dronke is an extreme purgacon'.[12] In 1665 William Harvey, hardly an unskilled physician, prescribed an electuary for Mrs Lucia Trout, who had a 'great soare under her chynn brake', consisting of sarsaparilla, senna, rhubarb, agaric, cassia, several other herbs, and two drams of 'the trochiske [lozenge] of vipers', all to be taken 'every newe and full moon'.[13] Like Macbeth's witches seventeenth-century medicine often added fauna to its flora. 'To cure the Thrush,' wrote Aubrey, 'take a living Frog, and hold it in a cloth, that it does not go down into the Child's Mouth, till it is dead; and then take another Frog.'[14] Not surprisingly, observers of these activities were sometimes sceptical. What use were doctors, asked Dekker during the plague of 1603: 'Their Phlebotomies, Losinges, and Electuaries . . . their Diacatholicons, Diacodions [laxatives], Amuletts, and Antidotes, had not so much strength to hold life and soule together, as a pot of Pinders Ale and a Nutmeg.'[15]

Medical knowledge improved during the sixteenth and seventeenth centuries. The Flemish physician Vesalius dissected human bodies and was responsible for important advances in anatomy. His works, published in the 1530s and 1540s, eventually undermined the entire Galenist system. Vesalius' work was continued in the next generation by Fabricius, a teacher of anatomy and physiology at Padua at the time William Harvey studied there. By the early seventeenth century human anatomy was being taught at Cambridge, albeit not very effectively. Harvey's fundamental work on the circulation of the blood came in the 1620s. A greater understanding of how the human body functioned was thus being gained, but progress in remedying things when they went wrong was much less impressive. Valuable work in surgery was done by Ambroise Paré during his service with the French army in the early sixteenth century. He discontinued the agonising practice of cauterising wounds with boiling oil and developed the use of ligatures for tying arteries following injury and amputations. He also designed surgical instruments and artificial limbs and made important contributions to obstetrics. But in the absence of antiseptics and anaesthetics, surgery remained very limited in its applications.

Some progress in the treatment of illnesses was achieved by the development of new drugs and careful diagnosis. Until the sixteenth century medicine had relied on a vegetable-based pharmacopoeia supplemented by the odd viper or toad. However, Paracelsus, the Swiss-born physician-cum-astrologer-cum-alchemist, added sulphur, lead, mercury and also laudanum to the range of drugs available. Mercury was found to be particularly effective in treating syphilis, a disease that proved something of a landmark in medical history, since it sent doctors stumbling towards an understanding of how infections could be transmitted as well as treated. Another useful addition to the medical armoury was quinine, introduced into Europe from America by Jesuit missionaries in 1632. Mixed with water, rose water, lemon juice and other fluids, it was an effective antidote for fever. Quinine was the basis of the celebrated 'Sydenham drops', invented by the outstanding English physician Dr Thomas Sydenham, who had an extensive practice in post-Restoration London. Sydenham had considerable success in treating disease, largely because of the care with which he made his clinical observations. He was able to distinguish the symptoms of various kinds of illnesses and sought the causes of infections by associating particular diseases with particular conditions of climate and environment.

Until the medical profession began to understand the causes of disease it was like an eyeless, armless boxer when trying to combat the battalions of suffering. With the exception of syphilis, even the immediate causes of most maladies were not understood. The commonly accepted view was that diseases were caused by a 'miasma' or mist falling from the sky or arising from putrefaction within the earth. A poetic expression of the theory was given by Thomas Dekker, when writing of plague:

> Yet must we graunt that from the veines
> Of Rottenness and Filth, that reignes,
> O're heapes of bodies, slaine in warre,
> From Carrion (that indangers farre)
> From standing Pooles, or from the wombes
> Of Vaults, of Muckhills, Graves, & Tombes,
> From Boggs; from ranck and dampish Fenns,
> From Moorish breaths, and nasty Denns,
> The Sun drawes up contagious Fumes,
> Which falling downe burst into Rhewmes,
> And thousand malladies beside,
> By which our blood growes putrified.
> Or, being by windes not swept from thence,
> They hover there in cloudes, condense,
> Which suckt in by our spirits, there flies
> Swift poyson through our Arteries,
> And (not resisted) strait it choakes
> The heart, with those pestiferous smoakes.

The only modification of this view was that, ultimately, all things came from God:

> God in anger fills his hand
> With Vengance, throwing it on the land;
> Sure tis some Capital offence,
> Some high, high Treason doth incense
> Th' Eternall King, that thus we are
> Arraign'd at Deaths most dreadfull barre.[16]

The frequency with which complaints were voiced in London and other cities about the congested and noisome state of urban graveyards, sprang as much from the belief that rotting corpses were a prime cause of infection as from any objections on aesthetic grounds. As we have noted, in the eighteenth century both malaria and influenza were named on the strength of the miasmic theory. The same theory was at least partly behind the public health agitation of the 1840s; and it was still being seriously advanced in epidemiological writings at the end of the nineteenth century.

Apart from syphilis, the one major disease that medical science had begun to grapple with effectively before the nineteenth century was smallpox. Edward Jenner published his work on vaccination in 1798, although its effects were not felt until the nineteenth century. But much earlier in the eighteenth century inoculation—as opposed to vaccination—had been developed. There was a long folk tradition of exposing healthy children to mild attacks of smallpox, even of rubbing an infected pock on the arm of a healthy child in order to gain an immunity from a more severe infection in adult life. In 1714 an account of a method practised in Greece of inoculating patients with pus taken from pustules of smallpox sufferers was published in England and excited some discussion among medical men. The method gained more widespread publicity in 1721, when Lady Mary Wortley Montague, who had lived in Constantinople where smallpox was rampant, had her daughter inoculated; and in the following year the Princess of Wales had her two daughters inoculated, with some trepidation. Despite this fashionable patronage, the method did not at first become widely accepted. It was expensive—the patient usually required a week or two's nursing—and it was not without risk. However, the use of milder viruses from the 1740s reduced the dangers of dying from inoculation, and from the 1750s Poor Law authorities in some parishes began to pay doctors to carry out inoculations during epidemics of smallpox. In this way they hoped to reduce the costs of pauperism that arose from the deaths of breadwinners during epidemics. In the 1760s inoculation spread widely, largely through the efforts of a Nottinghamshire practitioner, Robert

Sutton, and his son David. By 1776 the Suttons and their associates claimed to have inoculated 300,000 people, many of them paupers whom they treated free of charge on condition that they had the monopoly of inoculating the remainder of the inhabitants of the parish. Others copied the methods of the Suttons, and inoculation became fairly common in the countryside and in some provincial towns, although much less so in London and the larger cities. Inoculation continued to be employed in the nineteenth century and was only gradually replaced by vaccination.

Smallpox remained a major cause of death throughout the eighteenth century, although its fatality rate fell. There is no agreement whether this was the result of inoculation or whether it was caused by a decline in the virulence of the disease itself. Probably some credit should be allowed to inoculation for erecting a small dam against the stream of death.

In general the medical profession was hindered in dealing with disease by a shortage of manpower and an overdose of ignorance. Into the void poured an army of empirics, astrologers, quacks, magical men, wise women, faith healers, witches, and others, equipped with traditional recipes, spells and incantations, talismans and tokens that in many cases probably did no more harm than more approved treatments and may, on occasion, have done a little good. The line between professional practice and folk medicine was, in any case, very ill-defined, except perhaps in London, where the College of Physicians kept a semi-monopolistic hold on the supply of doctors. Even in London it was possible to find 'empirics', men not formally licensed to practise medicine. These men sometimes enjoyed a considerable reputation, particularly if they obtained the patronage of some high-placed member of society. Such a man was Richard Napier, who 'was no Doctor, but a Divine and Practised Physicke' in the late sixteenth and early seventeenth centuries. His methods were hardly scientific. 'When a patient or Querant came to him, he presently went to his Closet to Pray. . . . He did converse with the Angel Raphael, who gave him the Responses, and told him to admiration the Recovery or Death of the Patient. His knees were horny with frequent Praying.'[17] Some empirics were simply men who did not adhere rigidly to orthodox medical teaching and who were ostracised by the profession as a result. Followers of Paracelsus, for example, found it difficult to gain acceptance from orthodox Galenist practitioners. Even William Harvey, a respectable pillar of the medical establishment, lamented that he 'fell mightily in his Practize' following the publication of his *Circulation of the Blood*, and that it was 'beleeved by the vulgar that he was crack-brained; and all the Physitians were against his Opinion'.[18]

Many empirics, however, were frauds out to make a profit from human suffering. During outbreaks of plague, empirics and quacks erupted almost as readily as the buboes of its victims. In 1603 many professional physicians retreated to the safety of the countryside, leaving the care of the city's sufferers to

a band of Desper-vewes, some fewe Empiricall madcaps (for they could never be worth velvet caps) turned themselves into Bees (or more properlie into Drones) and went humming up and downe, with hony-brags in their mouthes, sucking the sweetness of Silver . . . out of the poison of Blaines and Carbuncles: and these jolly Mountibanks clapt up their bils upon every post (like a Fencers Challenge) threatning to canvas the Plague, and to fight with him at all his owne severall weapons: I know not how they sped, but some they sped I am sure, for I have heard them band for the heavens, because they sent those thither, that were wisht to tary longer upon earth.[19]

They appeared again in 1625, hawking their useless

remedies, and were strongly in evidence in 1665, advertising 'infallible preventive pills against the plague' and 'sovereign cordials against the corruption of the air'. Handbills appeared on walls advertising 'An eminent High Dutch physician, newly come over from Holland, where he resided during the time of the great plague last year in Amsterdam, and cured multitudes of people that actually had the plague upon them.' Women, too, appeared among the quacks, including an 'ancient gentlewoman [who] gives advice only to the female sex'. One trickster advertised free advice, although the obligatory prescription that followed it cost half a crown. These and others plied a busy trade among the poor who purchased 'charms, philtres, exorcisms, amulets . . . to fortify the body with them against the plague'. Many of those same bodies were later 'carried away in dead-carts and thrown into the common graves of every parish with these hellish charms and trumpery hanging about their necks'.[20]

If the line between empirics and recognised practitioners were hazy, so was the division between doctors and surgeons on the one hand, and midwives and astrologers on the other. A few physicians were interested in midwifery in the sixteenth and seventeenth centuries, but 'men-midwives' were not generally accepted before the eighteenth century; the few that practised were sometimes obliged to grope blindly beneath the sheets. Midwives were supposed to receive episcopal licences after training with older, experienced women, but this form of regulation was utterly ineffective. Midwives often did more harm than good, and women in labour were often better off without them. William Harvey was an outspoken critic of inefficient midwifery:

The younger, more giddy, and officious Midwives are to be rebuked which when they hear the woman in travaile cry out for paine and call for help, lest they should seem unskilful at their trade, and less busie then comes to their share, by daubing over their hands with oyles, and distending the parts of the Uterus, do mightily bestirre themselves, and provoke the expulsive faculty by medicinal potions: so that being impatient of an competent expectation by their desire to hasten and promote the Birth, they do rather retard and pervert it, and make it an unnatural and difficult delivery.

'It is much happier with poor women,' concluded Harvey, 'where the Midwives help is never required.'[21] The techniques of obstetrics were advanced by Dr Peter Chamberlen in the second quarter of the seventeenth century, but he provoked the hostility both of midwives in London, who thought he was trying to monopolise their business, and of the College of Physicians, whom he offended by 'his style of clothing . . . [which] were more like the dress worn by the very gay young men at court',[22] than the 'quiet garments' of the Fellows of the College. For these and other offences he was eventually dismissed from his fellowship.

If medicine and midwifery existed in uneasy relationship, medicine and astrology were for centuries cosy bedfellows. That the heavenly bodies influenced the constitution of the earthly ones was a universally accepted axiom of medical science—indeed, astrological influences extended far beyond the sphere of medicine. There was commonly held to be a direct connection between the movements of the planets and human physiology. The moon controlled the phlegm, Jupiter and the sun the movements of the blood, Saturn the black bile, and Mars the yellow bile. It followed that astrology was a vital adjunct of diagnosis and prescription: the horoscope and the urine glass both were consulted. Astrological observations also determined the times most suitable for purging and bleeding and for the administering of medicines. Published almanacks, which enjoyed a wide circulation in the seventeenth century, frequently contained information designed to guide the reader in choosing the most propitious times for medical treatment.

Some astrologers enjoyed a wide quasi-medical practice and included highly placed members of society among their clients. The most flamboyant was probably Simon Forman, who practised in London in the late sixteenth and early seventeenth centuries; it is not clear whether his scandalous sexual reputation was a help or hindrance in obtaining female clients. Forman saw over a thousand clients a year at the end of the sixteenth century; William Lilly, who practised in the seventeenth century, handled about twice this number. Many customers, of course, came not in search of medical advice, but for information about lost goods, what careers to follow, how to pick the winner in a horse or dog race, and so on. But others had medical or psychological problems, including women who came seeking advice on pregnancy or barrenness. The medical institutions were generally sympathetic towards astrology in the sixteenth and early seventeenth centuries, and the College of Physicians numbered astrologers among its ranks. But its attitude was sometimes equivocal. Simon Forman was prosecuted by the College of Physicians on a number of occasions; on the other hand, the University of Cambridge awarded him the degree of MD and licensed him to practise medicine. There was an obvious element of rivalry as well as co-operation between astrology and medicine: 'That which many physicians could not cure or remedy with their greatest and strongest medicines, the astronomer hath brought to pass with one simple herb, by observing the moving of the stars.'[23] As the intellectual basis of astrology gradually became eroded during the seventeenth century, so the part it played in medicine slowly declined.

The bulk of medical care in pre-industrial England was dispensed in the form of traditional folk medicine. In practically all communities there were men and women renowned for their gifts of healing. 'Sorcerers are too common; cunning men, wizards, and white witches, which, if they be sought unto, will help almost all infirmities of body and mind,' wrote Robert Burton in 1621.[24] For the most part they relied on a mixture of herbs, ritual and psychology. They made extensive use of the medical properties of herbs and minerals, knowledge of which was passed from generation to generation. This knowledge was sometimes written down, as for example, in Nicholas Culpeper's *Physicall Directory*, first published in 1649 and still enjoying a vigorous life in the nineteenth century. Home-grown plants were supplemented by imported exotics. One of the most common of these was tobacco, which was popularly supposed to ward off plague. When the plague raged in London in 1665 the boys of Eton College 'were obliged to smoke in the school every morning'. One pupil later recalled that 'he was never whipped so much in his life as he was one morning for not smoaking'.[25]

The administration of medicine was frequently accompanied, and was sometimes replaced, by magical rituals. These were often simply the recitation of Latin prayers, followed by an order to the disease to cease. Sometimes the ritual was more elaborate. Apparently meaningless words might be written on a piece of paper by the healer, and worn by the sufferer about the person for a while before being burned. Charms were available for all occasions, for 'the staying of serpents, bleeding at the nose, blastings, inflammations, burnings with fire, scaldings with water, agues, tooth ache, cramps, stitches, prickings, ragings, achings, swellings, heart burnings, flowings of the head, etc.'.[26] Some healers worked by touch. Until the eighteenth century English monarchs treated sufferers of the King's Evil, a tubercular swelling of the lymph glands of the neck. Charles II alone touched over 90,000 sufferers during his reign. Queen Anne was the last sovereign to use the royal touch and numbered the infant Samuel Johnson among her patients. Healers by touch were also found further down the social scale, claiming to possess some divine gift of healing, stemming, perhaps, from being a seventh son of a seventh son.

Disease was frequently assumed to be the result of the patient being possessed by an evil spirit; the cure, therefore, lay in exorcising the evil. This was done by 'wise women' and 'cunning men', who trod a thin (and sometimes invisible) line, between exorcism and black magic, which was regarded as malevolent rather than benign. Wise women might achieve a cure by transferring the disease from one person to another. For example, in 1555 a mother who had a sick child was advised to 'cause herself to be in as ill a case as the said child then was (who was then likely to die) ere she could help her'.[27] In other cases the healer herself would manifest symptoms of the sufferer's ailment. Wounds were sometimes treated by anointing the weapon that caused them with an appropriate salve. A somewhat similar remedy for toothache was recommended by Aubrey: 'To cure the Tooth-ach, Take a new Nail, and make the Gum bleed with it, and then drive it into an Oak. This did cure Sir Willial Neal... a very stout Gentleman, when he was almost mad with the Pain, and had a mind to have pistoll'd himself.'[28]

That an intelligent man like Aubrey could trust in such a remedy is testimony to the strength of faith in magical cures and a measure of the failure of rational medical practice to provide relief for human suffering. But Aubrey also quoted with approval, when discussing touching for the King's Evil, Francis Bacon's cynical remark 'That Imagination is next Kin to Miracle-working Faith'.[29] Folk cures sometimes worked because they were believed to work. Some herbal preparations possessed therapeutic properties that were useful in treating certain conditions. Many ailments went away of their own accord, but who could deny that the charm worn round the neck or the rabbit's foot in the pocket did not play a part? Aches and pains often had a psychological rather than physical origin, and they therefore yielded to treatments in which the sufferer had confidence. Thus folk medicine in pre-industrial England had as much chance of relieving suffering as orthodox medical practice. Neither, however, was able to do much to stem the vast flood of disease that poured over England. Against plague, typhus, smallpox and the other major killers, medical men and magical women showed a common helplessness.

If diseases could not be effectively combated once they occurred, there was at least a chance of preventing their outbreak or curbing their spread. Arising directly from the belief that rotting and odorous matter was a source of infection, public authorities throughout the sixteenth, seventeenth and eighteenth centuries struggled to keep their cities clean, or at least clean enough to meet the unexacting standard of the time. These efforts usually focused on the water supply and street-cleansing operations, and also on the regulation of noxious crafts. In addition, practically every town of any size took specific measures during outbreaks of plague to contain the spread of the contagion.

In pre-industrial England the rivers, springs and wells provided the water used for washing, cooking, sanitation, transport and industrial purposes. In the growing towns the demand for water put great strains on natural supplies, and municipal authorities were forced to control their use and seek alternative supplies. In London the New River was constructed between 1609 and 1613 to bring water from near Ware in Hertfordshire to Islington over forty miles away. This enterprise was undertaken mainly under private sponsorship, but the city authorities were also active. Similar operations were carried out in the provinces: the city of Worcester, for example, spent £200 in the early seventeenth century on bringing water from country areas to cisterns within the city boundary.

The main problem facing municipalities was to balance the claims of competing users of water and particularly to ensure that there were sufficient supplies of clean drinking water. The worst threat to supplies came from domestic users who dumped their household refuse into drains, ditches, rivers and roads, from where it quickly found its way into sources of drinking water. However, the efforts of city authorities were directed more against industrial users than against householders, and especially against craftsmen such as leather workers and butchers who used large quantities of water in their trades. In many towns these trades were forced to occupy sites downstream, beyond the city boundary. In London a combination of municipal regulations and high rents had forced the tanners out of the city proper into Bermondsey as early as the fourteenth century. In 1550 the city authorities of Northampton—a city that has suffered from inadequate water supplies for much of its history—ordered that 'No glover [shall] washe no skinnes in the hyghe Ryver nor without the west bridge nor drye any woll upon the grasse in the Fote medow, but shall wash ther Skynnes in the pyt under the brydge next unto Dalington.'[30] Forty years later the borough of Castle Combe told its glovers not to 'washe any skynnes nor cast any other fylth or soyle in the water runninge by his house'. Paradoxically, the odour of the tanyard was regarded as providing a protection against plague; and when the disease attacked Nottingham in 1666 the population flocked to the river Leen, where the tanyards were, for a whiff or two of the prophylactic smell. Butchers, too, were a nuisance. At the end of the fifteenth century it was alleged that butchers in London were creating 'unclene and putrified waters' by dumping 'bloode and other fowle thynges, by occasion of the slaughter of bestes and scaldying of swyne' into rivers. The same problem still existed almost two centuries later when the Fleet river was in a polluted state because of the 'constant injection of the inhabitants thereabouts of great quantities of filthy garbage from slaughter-houses and such like places'.[31]

Streets, like rivers, were rubbish-dumps as well as thoroughfares. Industrial craftsmen and householders were as much a problem here as with rivers; in 1582 the borough of Northampton was forced to instruct its leather works, not for the first time, not 'to cast any dead horse, mare, or gelding, or any dog, hog, or other such carrion, on the streets, ways, ditches, or any ground of the town save in the Marehold'.[32] The marehold was to be cleaned out once a year. Many householders kept a dung-heap in the back yard. In the countryside these were valuable sources of manure for the farmland and did not create a serious nuisance, but country ways caused problems when practised in the cities. Human excrement was regularly thrown into the open gutters running down the centres of city streets. This arrangement prevailed even in well-to-do districts. When Lord Keeper Guildford moved into a large house in Chancery Lane in London during the 1670s he found 'a small well in the cellar, into which all the drainage of the house was received'. When the well was full, it was pumped 'into the open kennel [channel] of the street', creating such a stench that it offended 'not only his lordship, but all the houses in the street, and also passengers that passed to and fro in it'. The sanitary arrangements of the neighbouring houses were similarly 'obnoxious to the same inconveniences', but their occupants refused to be connected to a newly constructed sewer until Guildford persuaded the city authorities to force them to bear the cost. The outcome was so pleasing that his neighbours 'thanked his lordship, as for a singular good done them'.[33] Officialdom did what it could by employing scavengers and dung-farmers to remove the worst of the filth from the streets, and even extended its activities to interiors of houses. Thus, in the late sixteenth century, curriers in the city of London were ordered to devote half of every Saturday to cleaning themselves and their premises. Some credit should be given to city governors for preventing their towns from being completely buried under mountains of muck. Until the later eighteenth century at least the provincial towns maintained a modicum of cleanliness; but after 1750 their efforts were frequently overwhelmed by the growth of population.

Every town was provoked into a frenzy of activity when plague broke out. There was much to be done: the dead to be buried in mass graves, the poor to be maintained, property to be protected; but, above all, the contagion to be contained. Although the cause of plague was not understood, it was observed that it spread rapidly in the densely populated areas. A policy of quarantine and containment therefore presented itself as the most obvious course of action—indeed, the only possible course in the absence of any alternative effective solution. The most elaborate arrangements were developed in London, where the plague problem was most serious, although all urban areas were forced to take preventive measures from time to time. Regulations for the control of plague in the capital evolved gradually during the sixteenth and early seventeenth centuries, and by the middle of the seventeenth century London possessed a comprehensive set of controls. In 1665 these were reissued as *Orders Conceived and Published by the Lord Mayor and Alderman of the City of London concerning the Infection of the Plague*.[34] These orders provided for the appointment of 'searchers' in every parish to seek out cases of infection and to see that infected houses were shut up. They further enjoined that 'to every infected house there be appointed two watchmen, one for every day, the other for the night; and that the watchmen have a special care that no person go in or out of such infected houses whereof they have the charge, upon pain of severe punishment'. Women searchers, physicians and surgeons were also appointed 'for the cure and prevention of the infection', and householders were obliged to give notice of cases of plague occurring in their houses. Persons within infected houses were to be confined there, together with the sick, usually for a period of a month. Burials were to to take place between sunset and sunrise, without mourners; graves were to be six feet deep. Other regulations prohibited the sale of bedding and clothing from infected houses and dealt with the cleaning of streets and the airing of hackney carriages. All contaminated houses were to be marked with a red cross one foot high and emblazoned with the doleful legend 'Lord, have mercy upon us'. As an additional precaution, beggars were ordered from the streets, theatres were closed, public feastings banned, and 'disorderly tippling in taverns, ale-houses, coffee-houses and cellars' forbidden after 9 p.m.

Formidable as such regulations appeared on paper, they did little good. Plague deaths were frequently concealed by frightened householders, and at the height of epidemics there simply was not enough manpower to cope. In 1665 the aldermen of London appointed several physicians, at least one of whom died of plague. The city pest-house, established during the epidemic of 1593, handled some cases of plague, but it was helpless in the face of large-scale infection. Even had the regulations issued in 1665 been fully implemented, they would have failed to curb the epidemic, for they were based on a fundamentally false assumption. It was assumed that plague was highly infectious, whereas, in fact, the bubonic form was one of the least infectious of the major diseases. Only rarely did plague pass from man to man. For the disease to spread through a human population, that population had to be in close contact with infected rats. If people moved away from an infected region, they did not take plague with them unless they harboured infected rat fleas in their clothing or baggage. The best defence against plague was retreat, as many of the more wealthy, at least, instinctively realised. Quarantine merely made things worse by forcing healthy people to live in the closest proximity to human sufferers carrying infected rat fleas. In London the worst affected districts were always the very poor overcrowded parishes, and a man like Pepys could walk through the business and fashionable residential quarters of the city with comparative immunity.

Thus neither private medicine nor public health offered much protection against the mortal forces afflicting pre-industrial man. The only real defences against disease were wealth, luck and common sense. The poor were more vulnerable than the rich: they lived in worse conditions, they were worse fed, worse dressed, and dirtier. Luck—or fate—was something over which man had little control, although prayer, charms and due attention to the movements of heavenly bodies were thought to help in picking a path through the hazards of life. As to common sense, there was a good deal an individual could do to reduce the risks of ill-health, although, again, the wealthier were better placed than the poor. Andrew Boorde, the Tudor physician, offered three pieces of good advice to his readers. 'Permyt no common pyssing place to be about the house.' This was more difficult to achieve in the towns than in the countryside, for in urban communities houses and tenaments were huddled so closely together that the privy could not easily be banished to the bottom of the garden. 'Ryse with myrth', advised Boorde, 'and remember God . . . and washe youre handes and wrists, your face and eyes and your teethe with cold water. . . . When dressed walke a mile before youre brake faste.' Good health, it might be argued, was a prerequisite for such a régime rather than a consequence. Above all, according to Boorde, 'Abstynence . . . is the moste beste and the payfytest mydycyne . . . to do sicke men pleasure and profyt . . . and whole men to preserve themselves from syckness.'[35] For the very wealthy, suffering from the ravages of over-indulgence, this was excellent counsel. Unfortunately, the bulk of the population in pre-industrial England suffered from the consequences of malnutrition rather than over-eating. For them abstinence was a condition forced on them by poverty, and it added to their vulnerability to illness of all kinds. Ultimately, it was the rising standards of living created by industrialisation that contributed to the lifting of the burden of disease. It was also the wealth created by industrialisation that eventually aided the development of medical science and so provided the defences against the many ailments that had for centuries plagued mankind.

# 6

## Violence and Death

A GREAT deal of death in pre-industrial England was violent in the sense that there was little of the genteel slipping away from life amid the full comforts of medical science that is characteristic today. There were few more violent ways of dying than from many of the manifestations of natural death; even the thought of plague struck terror into Thomas Dekker:

> A stiffe and freezing horror sucks up the rivers of my bloud: my haire stands on end with the panting of my braines: mine eye-balls are readie to start out, being beaten with the billowes of my teares: out of my weeping pen does the inck mournefullie and more bitterly than gall drop on the pale-faced paper, even when I thinke how the bowels of my sicke country have bin torne.[1]

If other diseases failed to stir literary men to purple prose, it was not because they were pallid, insignificant visitors. To die in the high fever of typhus or smallpox, from the 'griping of the guts', or to be hounded from life by the pangs of hunger, was scarcely less brutal than perishing from plague. But there were other forms of violence adding to the onslaughts of natural death. Men died in battle, paid the penalty of breaking the law, or were the victims of homicide or accident. In these ways unnatural death was added to the toll of mortality from natural causes.

Violence was a general feature of pre-industrial society.

Personal quarrels, disputes over property, arguments about politics, and even more about religion, led to bloodshed and sometimes to death. England was, as Professor Elton has remarked of the reign of Henry VIII, a 'rough, superstitious, excitable and volatile society'.[2] The occasions for blood-letting were endless, whether they were drunken brawls, matrimonial quarrels or economic disputes. In the countryside uncertainties about field boundaries or unreasonable claims for tithes from the clergy caused endless friction which sometimes flared into violence. In towns clashes occurred between rival groups of craftsmen, and fights broke out between opposing bands of apprentices. Altercations often arose between parties who had made unwritten contracts and who could not agree subsequently on the terms. Economic hardship was at the bottom of much aggression. 'The matter of seditions is of two kinds,' wrote Francis Bacon in the early seventeenth century 'much poverty and much discontentment,' and he went on to add that 'the rebellions of the belly be the worst'.[3] Tudor and Stuart governments were uncomfortably aware that a combination of economic distress, religious fervour and political disaffection was the stuff of bloody rebellion and violent death.

The reasons why personal quarrels, economic deprivation, or differences of opinion over religion or politics so often took a violent turn were various. The regular processes of the law for settling disputes must have seemed to many people too remote, too slow, or too expensive, and aggrieved parties therefore frequently took the law into their own hands. Throughout the period political decision-making was confined to a small group within society, a situation that probably failed to encourage respect for law and order among the masses. The widespread habit of wearing daggers and swords meant that a rush of temper was all too often followed by a rush of blood. There was no regular police force to curb acts of aggression and, until the end of the seventeenth century, no standing army which the government could use for restoring peace in times of rebellion.

In at least two spheres the government itself sanctioned violence and violent death as instruments of policy. In common with all European powers throughout the sixteenth, seventeenth and eighteenth centuries, England used war as a means of securing political, religious and economic goals. And, perhaps to a greater extent than in some other nations in western Europe, capital punishment was an established part of the penal system. The battlefield and the gallows added, albeit marginally, to the burden of death in pre-industrial England. By setting such examples, the government encouraged the use of violence by private citizens: when the state itself resorted to physical force as a means of achieving political or social goals, it was hardly likely that individuals would practise pacifism with their neighbours.

'War', Sir George Clark has written of the seventeenth century, 'was not a mere succession of occurrences but an institution, a regular and settled mode of action, for which provision was made throughout the ordering of social life. It was an institution in the sense that it was defined and arranged for by various prevailing systems of law, and also in a wider sense: the structure of society implied it would occur.'[4] Statesmen spoke as if peace was normal, yet they acted as though war was the usual relationship between nations. Distinctions were made between civil and foreign wars, and also between just and unjust wars: civil wars, involving 'blood against blood', fell into the latter category, while wars against the Infidel were regarded as more 'just' than strife between Christian kingdoms. Yet practically no voice was ever raised against the idea of war itself as a means of policy, or against the practice of devoting the human and material resources of the country to the pursuit of war. During the early sixteenth century war was used by kings and princes to achieve their dynastic ambitions. By the later sixteenth century these dynastic goals had usually hardened into those of the state or nation, for, in practice, ruling families identified their own interests with those of the peoples they governed. From the middle of the sixteenth century wars were also fought for religious reasons, and religious conflicts became characteristic of European history for the next century. Dynastic and religious aims were frequently overlaid by economic objectives, and these became increasingly dominant during the seventeenth and early eighteenth centuries.

It is difficult to decide how often England was at war before the nineteenth century, for so often hostilities took place before war was formally declared, and sometimes a declaration of war was not followed by actual fighting. Between the accession of Henry VIII and the death of Elizabeth I the country was formally at war for something like forty years. During the first half of the sixteenth century the main enemy was France, often in alliance with an even nearer adversary, the Scots; the main issues involved were essentially dynastic. In the second half of the century the Spanish gradually emerged as the villains in the eyes of the English, principally because of clashes over religion, although there were also rivalries over the economic resources of the New World. From the 1560s England was engaged in a thinly disguised undeclared war with Spain. This cold war flared into open hostilities in 1585 that lasted for the next twenty years. A peace with Spain in 1604 ushered in four decades free of foreign involvement, interrupted only briefly by war with Spain in 1624 and with France the following year. In the 1640s England fell disastrously into war, first in Ireland in 1641, and then into the great Civil War. In 1652–54 England was at war with the Dutch, the first conflict in which issues of trade and colonisation were paramount, followed by war—also largely commercial in motive—with Spain.

In the later seventeenth century England was a major economic and political power in Europe and warfare

E

became an almost unceasing background to English life. Two wars with the Dutch in 1665–67 and 1672–74 were fought mainly on the seas, but gradually England was sucked into continental struggles and virtually the whole of the 1690s was taken up with the struggle against France. A brief peace between 1697 and 1702 was followed by the War of the Spanish Succession that involved England in massive land campaigns until 1710 and did not finally end until 1714. Peace proved an ephemeral possession, however. As well as the brief campaign against the Jacobites in 1715–16, there was war with Spain in 1718–20, 1727–29 and 1739–48. In 1744 France formed an alliance with Spain against England in the War of the Austrian Succession. The Seven Years' War occupied the years 1756–63. In 1775 war broke out with the American colonies, and this conflict broadened into a wider dispute with France, Spain and Holland that was not finally settled until 1784. Finally, the eighteenth century ended with a war with France that commenced in 1793 and was not finally concluded until 1815.

Despite the frequency of war before the nineteenth century, its contribution to total mortality in the form of death directly sustained in the field of battle was small. Individual campaigns could, of course, claim large numbers, although it is remarkably difficult to obtain reliable statistics of casualties in battle. Flodden Field claimed the lives of 10,000 Scotsmen in 1513, but only a fraction of that number of Englishmen. The abortive attack on Corunna in 1589, led by Sir Francis Drake and Sir John Norreys, resulted in losses put variously at between 3,500 and 11,000. The bulk of these deaths were not battle casualties at all, but victims of disease or starvation; some 1,200 men, for example, died on the six-day march to the walls of Lisbon. Two years later Norreys commanded a force of 2,000 men in Brittany, half of whom failed to return home, although once again deaths through sickness and desertion outnumbered battle casualties. The first

Civil War of 1642–46, according to one historian, cost the lives of 100,000 Englishmen, but it is difficult to believe that more than a small fraction fell fighting. Most of the clashes between the Parliamentary and Royalist armies were skirmishes resulting in few deaths. In terms of fatalities, the most serious battle was Marston Moor in July 1644, when the combined deaths on both sides totalled 4,000. At Naseby in the following June losses were also counted in thousands rather than hundreds. More typical, though, was the battle of Roundway Down in July 1643, when the Royalists destroyed a Parliamentary army of 4,500 men; only 600 were killed, and the rest were captured.

In the late seventeenth century the greatest number of deaths were sustained in the land battles of the 1690s. At the Battle of Steenkirk in July 1692, 3,000 Englishmen and Scotsmen lost their lives, and in the following year there were 16,000 British casualties, killed, wounded and captured at Neerwinden. By contrast, the naval engagements of the Dutch wars of the 1660s and 1670s resulted in much smaller losses. Thus the abortive attack on Dutch shipping in Bergen harbour in 1665 cost the English 400 men. For the eighteenth century, the only overall estimates of casualties come from the French wars at the end of the century. According to one source, during the twenty years of fighting the British army lost 25,000 men who were killed or died from their wounds, and another 219,000 died from disease. Naval losses were 7,000 killed in action, 14,000 killed in shipwrecks and fire or by drowning, and 72,000 from disease or accident.

There were three reasons why deaths in battle were few in spite of the great frequency of war: armies were small before the late seventeenth century, the means of killing were inefficient, and accident and disease carried off so many that relatively few were spared to perish by force of arms. In the sixteenth century commanders were rarely able to field forces exceeding 20,000 men, and

armies were usually much smaller than this. The size of
armies grew during the seventeenth and eighteenth centuries. During the English Civil War the combined armies
of both sides totalled at most 120,000—140,000, including
infantry and cavalry. During the wars of the 1690s the
size of the British army increased rapidly from 8,000 to
90,000 men; it formed part of a combined allied army
that totalled over 300,000 soldiers. Counting both the
army and navy, the total number of men in English pay—
not all of them were Englishmen—rose to a maximum of
186,000 in 1711 and then declined rapidly. For much of
the 1720s and 1730s the number of men in the armed
services fluctuated between 30,000 and 50,000. During
the 1740s the army and navy grew in size once more to
a peak of 136,000 in 1746, and there was even a fear that
losses caused by war were contributing to a decline in the
total population. After 1746 the armed forces were
reduced in size once more until they rose again during the
Seven Years' War to a maximum of 205,000. With the
return of peace, the army and navy dwindled to 50,000
men, but by the end of the War of American Independ-
ence they numbered nearly a quarter of a million. After
1793 the army and navy contained at least 200,000 men
a year, and in some years almost half a million; the average number of men in the army and navy was now in
excess of 330,000 year.

Thus until the mid-eighteenth century the fighting services made small demands on the population. An Elizabethan army of 20,000 men represented no more than
0·5 per cent of the population. At the end of the seventeenth century William III's army contained roughly 1·5
per cent of the population, but many of the troops were
Scots and Irish, so the effective proportion of the English
population was lower. The maximum proportion of the
population of England and Wales under arms during the
Revolutionary and Napoleonic Wars was about five per
cent, and the average proportion more like three per cent.

With only small fractions of the population serving in the army or navy at any one time, it follows that war made little direct contribution to mortality. During the Revolutionary and Napoleonic Wars the casualty rate in the British army was approximately six men killed in action for every thousand men on active service. Statistically, fighting was an utterly ineffective way of killing anybody.

It cannot be imagined that earlier centuries could improve on the record of the 1790s, for neither in tactics, technology nor the quality of manpower were armies well equipped to kill in large numbers. At the Battle of Crecy, fought in 1346, English bowmen admittedly managed to slaughter 10,000 Frenchmen with their sustained arrow-fire. But this was exceptional, and during the fifteenth century bows and arrows were supplanted as fighting weapons by muskets and shot, even though the musket was an inferior weapon to the bow in every respect, except possibly in its intimidating noise. Bows were still in occasional use throughout the sixteenth century, but in the hands of untrained men or in the wrong situation they were ineffective. Thus, when the English laid siege to Leith in 1560, only one Scottish defender was hit by an arrow—the bow was never a good siege weapon—and he suffered greater agonies from the surgeon than from the arrow-head.

Although pikes and muskets were firmly established in most European armies by 1500, they were fearsomely cumbersome and inefficient. Muskets in particular required a clutter of supporting paraphernalia. In addition to the musket itself, the user required a flask of powder, a box of touch-powder, a bag of bullets, several yards of slow match for igniting the powder, a steel and flint to light the match, wadding, and a ramrod. To fire the musket, powder was put into the barrel, followed by the bullet and wadding to keep it in place; too little powder and the ball dribbled out of the barrel; too much and the whole gun blew up to the mortal peril of its operator. Muskets were highly inaccurate, their rate of fire was slow, and they soon overheated. To protect the users from the attacks of advancing cavalry, musketeers were arranged within a protective square of pikemen carrying wooden pikes eighteen feet long and tipped with metal. There might be as many as three thousand pikemen in these thickets, and the length of their pikes was enough to make the lances of the cavalrymen ineffective. The cavalry were therefore reduced to riding close enough to fire a pistol, even more inaccurate than a musket except at closest range, and then retreating. Since massed bodies of pikemen were difficult to manoeuvre, war became static and armies rarely clashed. The one major advantage that pikes and muskets offered to the commanders was that they made the best use of ill-disciplined, untrained peasants taken from civilian life by compulsory musters.

Weapons, tactics and fighting efficiency all slowly improved during the sixteenth and seventeenth centuries. Dutch, and later Swedish, commanders developed the use of small, mobile battalions of infantry and improved the ratio of pikes to guns, tactics that eventually became general throughout Europe. The fire power and accuracy of muskets improved and artillery was more frequently used, although it had been introduced long before the sixteenth century. It was of little use in open battle, for experienced soldiers 'upon [the artillery] giving fire do but abase themselves on their knee till the volew be passed'.[5] But the artillery was effective against fortified positions and was used during the Thirty Years' War and by both sides during the English Civil War. The biggest gun in use in the seventeenth century was the culverin, which could fire balls weighing 16–20 lb up to an extreme range of 2,100 paces. The cavalry, too, was eventually adapted to the new weapons and, armed with carbines, pistols and swords, became once more an effective offensive force.

In spite of these improvements, the glory of death in

battle remained an elusive honour. Not so death from disease while serving with the army or navy. In the Revolutionary and Napoleonic Wars soldiers stood over seven times as much chance of dying from disease or accident as they did of being killed by the enemy. The situation had been little different in earlier periods. In Thomas Dekker's *Dialogue betweene Warre, Famine, and the Pestilence*, published in 1604, Pestilence mocked at War:

Warre, I surpasse the furie of thy stroake,
Say that an Army fortie thousand strong,
Enter thy crimson lists, and of that number,
Perchance the fourth part falls, markt with red death?
Why, I slay fortie thousand in one Battaile,
Full of blew wounds, whose cold clay bodies looke
Like speckled Marble.
As for lame persons and maimed soldiers
There I outstrip thee too; how many Swarmes
Of bruised and crackt people did I leave,
Their Groines sore pierst with pestilentiall Shot:
Their Arm-pits digd with Blaines and ulcerous Sores,
Lurking like poysoned Bullets in their flesh?[6]

As we have seen, plague and typhus accompanied much of the military campaigning of the 1640s and 1650s, causing high mortality among the soldiers and also among the civilian population unfortunate enough to be in the way. Sickness among the troops or sailors sometimes put a complete stop to operations. For example, it proved impossible for William III to mount an attack on the joint forces of James II and the French in Kinsale harbour in Ireland in 1689 because the English fleet at Plymouth and the supporting troops were crippled by sickness caused by bad food and beer. In one squadron alone there were 530 deaths and over 2,000 cases of illness. Six years later an attack on the French-held island of Hispaniola by 1,300 troops failed because 1,000 of the attackers died of disease.

Whenever a large body of men were collected together sickness was almost inevitable because of the primitive state of sanitation and the inadequate provisions for health and hygiene. Surgeons served with armies, but their duty was to tend the wounded rather than the sick. During the Irish campaigns at the end of the sixteenth century, for example, dysentery—the 'Irish ague'—caused greater havoc among the English than anything the Irish soldiery could contrive. In 1600, when a church by Loch Foyle was converted into a hospital, it was inundated by 'incredible seas of sick and wounded men'. It was therefore suggested that the sick, who had only a one in ten chance of survival, should be excluded and that all medical attention should be concentrated on the wounded, whose chances of recovery were greater. All too often illness among the troops was accepted with an air of resignation. If they served in the Mediterranean or Caribbean, their commanders expected them to die of the heat and the food; if in the Low Countries, Scotland or Ireland, then of the cold and the damp. As one fatalistic and probably not very competent army doctor lamented during the Civil War,

> What is the physician or surgeon but dame Nature's hand maid to be aiding and assisting to her, but the great God of heaven has ordained and appointed several diseases which are incident to men, and that have to attend them one Death, who does and will prevail, notwithstanding the most excellent means which the wisest physician or surgeon may use in the world, and this we may see by daily experience.[7]

The risks of death from disease while serving in the army and navy increased during the seventeenth and eighteenth centuries as armies became larger. As they grew so did the problems of supplying them with food and disposing of their waste. The normal campaigning diet in the seventeenth century was bread and cheese:

'Nothing is more certain . . . that in the late wars both Scotland and Ireland were conquered by timely provisions of Cheshire cheese and biscuit,' reminisced an officer who had served in Cromwell's campaigns.[8] The navy especially suffered from the lack of fresh food, and the fighting effectiveness of the whole fleet was imperilled in the 1690s by the ill-health of its sailors. But at least the navy could dispose of its refuse and its dead in the sea, whereas armies had to camp among their excreta and get rid of their dead as best they could.

In a narrow sense, therefore, death in battle was the fate of the foolhardy and the unlucky; more likely was death from disease picked up while on campaign. Fortunately for the English, most of their wars were fought on foreign soil or at sea, and the country was thus spared that great loss of civilian life that occurred, for example, in Europe during the Thirty Years' War as advancing and retreating armies spread disease and devastated crops over vast tracts of the countryside. For the ordinary Englishman there were greater risks attached to the law than to war. Until the eighteenth century death at the end of a rope was more likely than death at the end of a pike or from a fatal wound inflicted by the ball of a musket.

Just as war was an accepted form of institutionalised violence, so violence was enshrined in the penal system and accepted by society as a normal means of enforcing law and maintaining order. Capital punishment was used in England for an astonishing range of offences. 'There is probably no other country in the world in which so many and so great a variety of human actions are punishable with loss of life as in England,' wrote Sir Samuel Romilly in 1810, looking back on the tangled thicket of capital statutes that had grown up during the eighteenth century.[9] In the 1820s there were roughly 220 or 230 capital statutes in operation, nearly 200 of which had been enacted during the eighteenth century. In 1688 there had been only about

fifty capital statutes, and in early Tudor England approximately twenty. But merely to enumerate the number of
laws providing for the death penalty does not give a full
indication of the risks accompanying criminal activity,
because many capital statutes were wide in their scope
and could be made even wider by the interpretation given
to them by the courts. The most notorious example was
the so-called Waltham Black Act passed in 1722, initially
for three years, but which was made permanent and not
repealed until 1823. The immediate object of the act was
to deal with a band of robbers in Waltham Forest, Hamp-
shire, who blackened their faces to disguise their identi-
ties. But the act was so loosely worded and so broadly
interpreted that it extended the death penalty to more
than fifty offences which might be committed by any one
of seven categories of persons—accomplices, accessories,
and so on. Thus there were over 350 varieties of offences
that might fall within the ambit of this single statute.

The range of offences carrying the death penalty was
enormous, stretching from high treason to theft of
property valued at more than twelve pence. Broadly
speaking, capital offences fell into four main groups: high
treason; other crimes against the state, such as defrauding
the public revenues (for example, by smuggling); crimes
against the person, such as homicide, maiming and sexual
offences; and a galaxy of offences against property,
including burglary, larceny, forgery, arson and piracy.
Although all these types of crime carried the death
penalty throughout the sixteenth, seventeenth and eighteenth centuries, offences against property were mainly
responsible for the large increase in capital statutes from
the end of the seventeenth century. No single reason
adequately explains this increase. The law exacted severe
penalties partly in order to counter the liberal bias of legal
procedures; for example, the jury system tended to work
in favour of the accused, and torture was no longer used
in the English legal system in order to obtain information

against accused persons. The absence of a police force no doubt heightened the sense of insecurity among citizens and so encouraged a strict penal code; but this was no less true of the sixteenth and seventeenth centuries than of the eighteenth. The growing wealth of the country during the eighteenth century may have led to a greater severity in the law where property was concerned: 'Commerce itself . . . is the fruitful mother of crimes of theft in all their varieties,' wrote the *Quarterly Review* in 1812,[10] implying that a greater protection from the law was needed. However, this explanation is not totally convincing. The eighteenth century was no doubt wealthier than the sixteenth, but this fact alone does not necessarily imply that there were more crimes against property per head of population. There is abundant evidence of widespread thieving in Tudor England, which certainly had no better methods of policing than the eighteenth century. The increasing harshness of the statute book in protecting property during the eighteenth century, therefore, still requires an explanation. All that can be said is that capital offences multiplied without provoking any serious public debate.

Although the eighteenth century piled up capital statutes to a greater degree than in earlier years, it does not follow that the law was enforced more severely; on the contrary, the chances of acquittal or commutation of sentence grew greater during the eighteenth century. 'If one were to mark out the period of greatest severity in modern English law,' one authority has written, 'the sixteenth and seventeenth centuries would undoubtedly form the central area. The non-clergyable felonies had already piled up, whereas evasion of the statutes did not occur to any extent until the eighteenth century.'[11] There is some slight statistical evidence to support this statement. Of nearly a thousand people accused of various felonies in the county of Essex during the last forty years of the sixteenth century, 21 per cent ended up on the gallows.

By contrast, at the turn of the seventeenth and eighteenth centuries the death sentence was carried out on roughly seven per cent of all persons committed for trial on the Home Circuit (Hertfordshire, Kent, Surrey and Sussex); by the third quarter of the eighteenth century less than five per cent of accused persons were executed, and by the end of the century only about four per cent.

There were various ways of avoiding the gallows, even when charged with a capital offence. An ancient method was to claim benefit of clergy. This was the right to be exempt from trial by the secular courts, or from sentences for first offences imposed by such courts, and was originally enjoyed by all who could read. But with increasing frequency the law established non-clergyable offences during the sixteenth and seventeenth centuries, thus blocking this particular bolt-hole. However, there were others. For example, when a charge was made, it might be thrown out by a grand jury appointed to decide whether there was a case to answer even before it came to trial. During the eighteenth century this happened more and more often with alleged capital offences. Even when cases actually went to trial, eighteenth-century courts tended to take a very formalistic view of indictments. Thus a mis-spelling of a defendant's name, or a minor error in stating the location of the alleged offence might result in the case being thrown out by the judge. During trials for grand larceny the charge might be reduced to petty larceny, not carrying the death penalty, by the judge or jury, or sometimes by the prosecution itself. Instances of 'pious perjury', whereby stolen goods were formally valued at less than forty shillings or twelve pence, depending on the charge, were common even when property of considerable value was involved. Finally, after conviction there was always the chance that a capital sentence would be reduced to one of transportation or imprisonment. Less than half the death sentences passed in London and Middlesex in the second half of the eighteenth century were actually

carried out. At the beginning of the eighteenth century
the risks of actually being executed if convicted of a
capital offence on the Home Circuit was one in two; by
the end of the century it was one in four.

Leniency in practice was the judicial system's way of
mitigating the severity of the law on paper. The courts
became more reluctant to convict during the eighteenth
century as the scope of capital punishment grew wider,
and it seems that the legal profession was perhaps in
advance of public opinion and the politicians who scattered capital statutes about in such profusion. The lack
of comparability between crimes carrying the death
penalty was partly responsible for the courts stopping
short of the full penalty of the law if they could. There
was also a growing feeling that extreme severity was in-
consistent with common humanity. Most offenders were
young: ninety per cent of those executed in the London
area in 1785 were under twenty-one. As late as 1800 a
boy of ten was sentenced to death for 'secreting notes',
although the sentence was commuted. There were
occasional instances of the death sentence being passed
on young children, which caused harrowing scenes in
court, not least among the lawyers themselves. By the end
of the eighteenth century, indeed, the indiscriminate range
of capital punishment was even beginning to provoke a
reaction in public opinion, and reform was in the air.

Hard figures of death upon the gallows are difficult to
come by. In a single year in Elizabethan England, 1598,
seventy-four people were sentenced to death in the county
of Devon, and on this basis one historian has suggested
that in the whole country there were about 3,000 death
sentences, of which actual executions 'could not have
been much below one-half or one-third'.[12] But one year
for one county is obviously a precarious base for estimat-
ing total executions. For one thing, the number of capital
sentences fluctuated from year to year: in Essex, for
example, there were seventeen capital convictions in

1559–60, whereas ten years later there were forty-nine; a further ten years later the number was thirty-six. Moreover, Devon was a large, well-populated county with, presumably, rather more executions a year than more sparsely populated regions. If there really were, say, a thousand executions a year in late Tudor England, capital punishment accounted for a little under one per cent of all deaths annually, assuming that the population numbered about four million, and that the normal death rate was around thirty per thousand.

All this is highly conjectural. What is more certain is that both the number and the rate of executions declined between the late sixteenth and the late eighteenth century. In Elizabethan England the number of executions in London and Middlesex seems to have averaged around 150 a year. By the reign of Charles I the figure was down to ninety, and in the middle decades of the seventeenth century to eighty-six. In the second half of the eighteenth century the average number of executions in London and Middlesex had fallen to thirty-four a year, but there were marked annual variations. From the point of view of the criminal classes, the healthiest year was 1759, when only six swung from the gallows; the worst year was 1785, when the law demanded final retribution from ninety-seven offenders. The general trend, however, was downwards. A dozen people died on the gallows in London and Middlesex in each year of the first decade of the nineteenth century. National figures are available only from 1805. In that year sixty-eight people were executed in England and Wales, and there was an average of sixty for the rest of the decade. Remembering the threefold increase in population that had taken place in England and Wales between the late sixteenth and early nineteenth century, it is evident that execution was becoming a rare form of death, in spite of the greatly increased range of capital statutes.

We have already seen that the capital statutes were

not being ruthlessly applied by the eighteenth-century courts. When the matter is examined a little more closely, we find that some offences practically disappeared from the list of executions over the years, either because the crimes were no longer committed or detected, or, if discovered, were no longer treated so severely; whereas other offences became, relatively, less lightly regarded. The most striking declines occurred in executions for treason and murder. The former, of course, tended to be highly erratic, increasing in number after some major upheaval such as a change of dynasty or attempted rebellion, but never very important in relation to the total number of executions. During the fifteenth century civil war was part and parcel of English political life, and noblemen unlucky enough to come out on the losing side were apt to be executed as traitors. But civil war gradually ceased to be part of the political scene during the sixteenth, seventeenth and eighteenth centuries—there were some striking exceptions—and the crime of treason became less common.

In the sixteenth century the headsman's axe took a periodic toll of high-born victims involved in dynastic or religious intrigue. For some families, like the Howards (Dukes of Norfolk), execution was almost a hereditary disease. Occasionally the crime of treason tripped up the humble as well. During the turmoils of the 1530s nearly nine hundred people were convicted of treason, of whom more than three hundred were executed. Twenty of them were victims of high dynastic and court politics; most of the rest were fairly humble people caught up in rebellions such as the Pilgrimage of Grace or convicted of supporting the papal supremacy. If we extend treason to include the crime of heresy, then between 1555 and 1558 the turn of the religious wheel sent nearly three hundred people to the stake. A few of them were church dignitaries but most of them were artisans, shopkeepers and people of low social rank. To take a purely political example, following the Northern Rising in 1569 more than five hundred people were executed. More than a century later, after Monmouth's rebellion in 1685, severe and indiscriminate punishment was meted out by Judge Jeffreys, resulting in 150 deaths and many more transportations. The Jacobite rising in 1715 produced a mere twenty-six executions. By the time that statistics became available in the eighteenth century, treason appears as an utterly insignificant reason for capital punishment. Of the 678 executions in London and Middlesex between 1749 and 1771, only one was for treason.

Murder, by contrast, was a more homely affair which did not fluctuate according to the vagaries of politics or religion. The fragmentary evidence that survives suggests that murder executions as a proportion of all executions declined during the eighteenth century. In late sixteenth-century Essex homicide—murder and manslaughter together—accounted for between 12 and 30 per cent of executions, but the actual number of cases was small. In 1689 eighteen murderers were hanged on the Home Circuit, representing 38 per cent of all executions, whereas in 1785 there was only one murderer in sixty-four executions. Taking a different area, London and Middlesex, seventy-two murderers were executed out of a total of 678 victims of the scaffold between 1749 and 1771, i.e. almost 11 per cent of the total; there were also fifteen executions for attempted murder. In the same area in 1785 there was only one murderer hanged out of a total of ninety-seven.

Three possible explanations for the declining rate of executions for murder suggest themselves. Possibly the crime of murder itself had declined by the eighteenth century, although there is no obvious reason why this should be so. Or perhaps the detection rate fell and murders and murderers were left undiscovered. Or perhaps society and the law were becoming laxer in their view of murder as a crime, with the result that the proportion of acquittals and commutations of sentence in cases of murder rose. For whatever reasons, during the eighteenth century the gallows took a smaller toll of the lives of those who had themselves taken the lives of others than it had done in earlier periods.

With the declining importance of treason and murder in total death sentences and the continuing small proportion of executions for other bodily offences such as rape and sodomy, the field was left clear for crimes against property. Even here there was a growing leniency. The only crime to which the courts did not soften their attitudes was that of forgery, perhaps because it was not easily detected and struck at the very foundations of the growing commercial prosperity of eighteenth-century England. The severity with which this offence was regarded was exemplified by the case of the unfortunate Rev. Dr Dodd, a fashionable London clergyman whose style of living ran in excess of his income. In 1777, in order to ease a pressing lack of liquidity, he attempted to obtain £4,300 by forging the signature of the Earl of Chesterfield, who had formerly employed him as a tutor. The attempt was soon discovered, Dr Dodd made full and speedy restitution, the Earl suffered the loss of not one penny, and it seems clear that Dodd never intended that he should. In the words of Dr Johnson, 'Be comforted: your crime, morally or religiously considered, has no very deep dye of turpitude. It corrupted no man's principles: it attempted no man's life. It involved only a temporary and reparable injury.' But this was cold comfort, for Dodd was arrested, tried, convicted and ultimately made the grim ride from Newgate to Tyburn, where he was hanged before a large and mainly friendly crowd numbering some thousands, with a squadron of troops tucked round the corner in case the exuberance of the onlookers got out of hand. A cynic later remarked that Dodd had committed 'a crime which, he must have known, can never afford even a hope for the royal mercy in this commercial country'.[13] But the case at least jolted public opinion into wondering whether death was not an excessive penalty, even for violating such established middle-class values as the sanctity of property and wealth.

Executions had an air of the circus about them. 'I did see Mr Chr. Love beheaded on Tower Hill in a delicate cleare day,' recorded John Aubrey. 'About half an hour after his head was struck off, the Clouds gathered blacker and blacker, and all that night and till next noon such terrible Claps of Thunder lightening and Tempest as if the Machine of the World had been dissolving.'[14] Attending a hanging was a regular London entertainment with especially large crowds flocking to the final acts of the more spectacular criminal cases. Earl Ferrers, a deranged gentleman hanged for the murder of his man-servant in 1760, drew a large audience, as did the hapless Dr Dodd. So great was the attendance at Tyburn in 1776 to witness the execution of the Perreau brothers for forgery that there were several casualties. A woman was pressed to death in the crush, a youth was killed by a fall from a coach on which he had clambered to get a better view; and three or four people were killed when a stand erected for spectators near the gallows collapsed. Executions remained public until well into the nineteenth century, ostensibly to increase the deterrent effect of capital punishment and also to add moral reprobation to the conviction. And, according to one nineteenth-century liberal arguing in favour of continuing the public spectacle, public executions prevented the state from secretly disposing of its opponents without trial.

There were several gallows around London—and many more in the provinces—but the most celebrated was Tyburn, three miles from Newgate, where the majority of convicted prisoners were housed. Until 1783, when the gallows was moved to Newgate, prisoners were taken in open carts through thronging crowds to the place of execution. If eye-witnesses are to be believed, English criminals died cheerfully, far from overcome by remorse, and behaving in a fashion hardly calculated to deter others from risking a similar end. The journey from Newgate to Tyburn often took two or three hours as the prisoner stopped for refreshment and exchanged boozy banter with friends and well-wishers. On arrival at Tyburn the condemned man was met by the hangman, to whom it was customary to present a gift for services rendered. Eighteenth-century hangmen were not noted for being upright and honest citizens themselves. Several were convicted of criminal offences, and one or two eventually experienced the practical consequences of their chosen craft. One hangman in 1738 was so drunk when attending to his duties that he tried to hang the accompanying clergyman as well as the convicted criminal. Until 1760 hanging was done simply by placing a noose around the convicted man's neck and whipping away the horse and cart. Several criminals could be dispatched simultaneously in this way. In 1760, however, technology took a hand at the cost of reduced productivity, and the 'drop', a trap door in a raised platform, was introduced.

Hanging was the usual manner of execution, but in 1752 the law established a variant of hanging. This was gibbeting—the hanging of a person in chains so that his body creaked and groaned at windy crossroads to the discouragement of others. Another elaboration was for the court to order that the body be delivered to surgeons for dissection. Both these additions were disliked by their recipients, perhaps because they seemed to deny, or at least delay, the possibility of Christian burial. For treason the law prescribed a bizarre ritual. The condemned man was dragged to the place of execution behind a horse and cart; in practice he was usually placed on a sledge. He was then hanged by the neck, but cut down while still alive, so that his bowels could be cut out and burned in his presence. Finally his head was cut off and his body quartered and usually put on display as a warning to others. This punishment was commuted to beheading in the case of peers, although the sentence of beheading was not officially known to English law. By the eighteenth century, however, the more gruesome parts of the punishment were a little too strong for popular taste and were abandoned. For women disembowelling and quartering were dispensed with because of 'the decency due to their sex', and burning substituted instead. The last woman to be burned in England for high treason was Elizabeth Graunt, a Baptist convicted in 1685 for sheltering a man involved in the Monmouth rebellion. But burning was still used during the eighteenth century for coining offences and for petty treason—the murder of a husband, master or mistress. As late as 1789 a woman was burned at Tyburn for coining; the sentence was abolished in the following year.

The spectacle of public executions was the epitome of the acceptance of violence in society before the nineteenth century. There were also forms of violence in society never officially countenanced by the state, though possibly encouraged by its willingness to use violence for its own ends. Rebellion, for example, was by definition opposed by authority, though resorted to often enough by its opponents. Duelling was a recognised way of salving slighted honour in some strata of society, but it was never acceptable to the state, which tried to stop it. And murder or manslaughter were always criminal acts that risked the penalties of the law.

It is impossible to know what contribution any of these causes of death made to total mortality, although it must have been very small. With the exception of the Great Rebellion of the 1640s, English rebellions were small-scale affairs with very few deaths. The Cornish rising of 1498, for example, caused only a couple of hundred fatal casualties, while the Lincolnshire rising and the Pilgrimage of Grace in 1536 were put down, almost without fighting, by negotiation and the execution of over two hundred of the participants. The potentially dangerous Northern Rising of 1569–70 was also suppressed with scarcely a blow struck in anger. Monmouth's rebellion of 1685 did see some skirmishes and one battle, at Sedgemoor. But rain, mud, incompetence and desertion did more to destroy Monmouth's army than death.

In addition to these national outbreaks of rebellion there were innumerable small-scale riots before the nineteenth century. Some had economic causes, but others were inspired by political motives or hostility to alien groups such as Jews, the Irish or Catholics. Occasionally they resulted in loss of life. Thus in 1715–16 the London 'mug house' riots between rival gangs of youths supporting the Hanoverian and Jacobite causes resulted in three deaths. Protests by woollen-weavers in London in 1719 against the importation and wearing of Indian calicoes in preference to woollen cloth resulted in one weaver being shot dead. Half a century later several people were killed when Spitalfields silk-weavers rioted in protest at attempts to establish weaving by machinery, which threatened their employment. In 1738 attempts by the government to curb the consumption of cheap gin—itself alleged to be the cause of many deaths—by imposing restrictions on its sale resulted in six informers being stoned to death in London in the space of seven months. A strike by coal-heavers in the port of London in 1768 led to the deaths of two strikers and a sailor in clashes with employers attempting to remove coal from the Thames lighters with blackleg labour. Politically inspired riots took a heavier toll. Approximately twenty people were killed or wounded during the St George's Field 'massacre' in 1768, following demonstrations in support of John Wilkes, the imprisoned radical MP. Much more serious were the anti-Catholic Gordon riots of 1780, which left 185 dead or dying of wounds, all of them apparently shot by the military called in to quell the trouble. Another twenty-five were hanged.

If the degree of concern of seventeenth-century governments is to be believed, duelling was a greater problem than rioting. According to the Attorney-General, Francis Bacon, writing in 1613, 'I consider the offence hath vogue only amongst noble persons or persons of quality.'[15] A duel was not merely a fight, such as might flare up at any time and lead to bloodshed, but a premeditated battle preceded by a challenge and with proper arrangement of weapons, seconds, and place of conflict. Most duels were fought in semi-secret, although there were several customary venues: in London Southampton Fields was known as a regular duelling ground, and the government, for all its anxiety about duelling, never prevented duellists from using it. The state's objection to duelling was twofold. One aspect was that it was a challenge to the state's own system of administering justice. The other was the waste of life it caused, especially among gentlemen whose aggressive instincts might be harnessed to military ends. A royal proclamation published in 1616 declared:

> The love and care Wee have towards the preservation of Our Subjects, and the keeping of Our Lande from being polluted with blood; doth make Us strive with the evill humors and depraved customes of the times, to reforme and suppresse them by Our Princely policy and Justice; to which end and purpose, We have by the severitie of Our Edict . . . put downe and in good part mastered that audacious custome of Duelles and Challenges, and have likewise by a statute made in Our time, taken away the benefit of Clergie in case of Stabbing and the like odious Man-slaughters: Wherefore it being alwayes the more principall in Our intention to prevent, than to punish, being given to understand of the use of Steelets, pocket Daggers, and pocket Dags and Pistols, which are weapons utterly unserviceable for defence, Militarie practise or other lawfull use, but odious, and noted Instruments of murther, and mischiefe; We doe straightly will and command all persons whatsoever that they doe not henceforth

presume to weare or carie about them any such Steelet
or pocket Dagger, pocket Dagge or Pistoll, upon
pains, of our Princely Indignation and displeasure,
Imprisonment and Censure in the Starre-Chamber;
And We doe likewise straightly forbid upon like paine
all Cutlers, or other persons, to make or sell any of the
said Steelets, pocket Daggers, pocket Dagges, or
Pistols.[16]

This was merely one of several statutes and proclamations designed to strengthen the ordinary common law
against murder and the carrying of offensive weapons. It
does not seem to have had much effect. There were at
least thirty-three deaths in duels in England in the decade
1610–19. Not all participants were gentlemen. In 1582
at Maldon in Essex two shoemakers who had been interrupted in a fist-fight decided to meet at dawn the next
day and finish the battle with pikestaves and daggers:
one was killed and the other fled. The Essex assizes
recorded the deaths of four people during the 1590s from
dagger, sword, or rapier wounds received during early-
morning conflicts; only one of the assailants was convicted. In 1598 the playwright Ben Jonson was convicted
following a fatal duel with Gabriel Spencer, but he
claimed benefit of clergy and was released. Duelling continued through the seventeenth century with little check
from the law, and there were notable cases of men in
high places being involved in duels and going unpunished;
among them were the Duke of Buckingham, a government minister, in 1668 and the Duke of Marlborough.
Only when the law gave adequate remedy to injured
reputation did duelling decline. 'Men's tongues growing
more virulent,' remarked the Lord Chief Justice in 1704,
'and irreparable damage arising from words, it has been
by experience found, that unless men can get satisfaction
by law, they will be apt to take it themselves.'[17]
The objections of government to the carrying of

weapons extended beyond their use in duels. They were, in the words of a proclamation of 1613, an 'inevitable danger in the hands of desperate persons'.[18] As John Aubrey observed, men carrying weapons were 'verie apt to doe Bloudy Mischiefes'. He gave examples. 'Edmund Wyld, Esq. had the misfortune to kill a man in London, upon a great provocation about A.D. 1644.' Aubrey himself had some narrow escapes. One night in 1673 he was 'in danger of being run through with a sword at Mr Burges' chamber in Middle Temple'. On another occasion 'I was in great danger of being killed by a drunkard in the street opposite Grayes-Inn gate—a gentleman whom I never saw before, but . . . one of his companions hindered the thrust.' During an election at New Sarum he was in 'danger of being killed by William, Earl of Pembroke, then Lord Herbert'. Aubrey described the first Earl, another William, who died in 1570, as a 'mad fighting fellow' who was on one occasion arrested at Bristol where he had 'killed one of the Sheriffes of the City'.[19]

Not only the upper classes resorted to swords and daggers. Fights between brawling sailors at Harwich in 1596 resulted in three deaths from sword or dagger wounds. A few years earlier an Essex labourer had used a sword to murder a man. But at these less exalted levels of society we find a more homely collection of weapons. Among homicides committed in Essex in the later sixteenth century, a farm servant was killed with a hedge bill and a pitchfork; a labourer killed a widow with a bodkin after first throttling her; another labourer killed two people with an axe; a butcher killed a woman, also with an axe—one of the tools of his trade, perhaps; a man was stabbed to death with a penknife; and a woman killed a man with a pikestaff. There were several cases of cudgels used with fatal results. An even more domestic weapon was used in 1763 by a London shoemaker who killed his wife (who sold milk) by throwing one of her own milk pails at her.

In this case, as in many others, murder was a family affair and the choice of weapon was dictated by what was immediately at hand. Even when the violence was more bizarre, murder in pre-industrial England, as today, was often a part of family life, if the word family is taken to include both lovers and servants as well as kin. In 1597 a man in Hadleigh, Essex, strangled his wife with a cord with which he had previously been whipping her. Also in late sixteenth-century Essex, a pregnant girl died from beatings inflicted by her boy-friend who was trying 'to make the child to be untimely born'.[20] The tables were turned by another pregnant woman who broke the neck of a man who was probably the cause of her condition. About 1560 an Essex spinster put her six-year-old son into an oven and suffocated him; she was pregnant again at the time. The Essex records reveal several cases of murder of spouse by spouse, children by parents—including an almost classic fairy-story instance of a brutal stepfather killing his stepdaughter by throwing her out of bed— servants by masters, and masters by servants. During the second half of the sixteenth century the Essex courts also dealt with five cases of poisoning, four of them committed by women; later, in the nineteenth and twentieth centuries, the use of poison appears to have been principally a female fashion.

It is easy enough to pile up examples of violent death arising from murder and manslaughter. The difficulty is to put them into perspective and to assess their importance, both to crime in general, and to mortality in particular. Some continental observers of eighteenth-century English society thought that, although Englishmen were frequently violent towards one another, their violence generally stopped short of homicide. Judging from the statistics of charges and convictions in London and Middlesex, in the eighteenth century, they may have been right. In the five years between 1710 and 1714 there were only four murder convictions in London. Of the ninety-seven people charged in London and Middlesex in 1785, only one was a murderer. When national figures became available, we find that in 1810 sixty-four people were committed for trial for murder in the whole of England and Wales. Seven years later there were eighty, out of a total of almost 14,000 committed for crimes of all kinds; there were also sixty-eight cases of manslaughter. For an earlier period, the figures collected for felonious cases heard before the Essex assizes in the later sixteenth century indicate that unlawful killings, at least those discovered and brought to trial, were small in total, and insignificant compared with other types of criminal activity. In five pairs of years between 1559 and 1602 the Essex assizes heard seventy-one cases of murder and homicide, out of a total of 965 felonious cases. An average of seven murders a year in one of the most populous regions of the country certainly does not suggest a surfeit of killing. To take another example, also from Essex, in the three villages of Hatfield Pereval, Boreham, and Little Baddow, together containing between 1,150 and 1,300 people, there were only four convictions for murder in the period 1560–99. We should expect at least 1,200 deaths from all causes during the same period in these communities (thirty deaths per thousand per year for forty years), balanced, of course, by a slightly bigger number of births. But before concluding that murder was practically an unknown crime, we should also reflect that only five villagers came before the courts for drunkenness; perhaps the law did not always catch up with instances of human depravity.

There was one category of murder which almost certainly went largely undetected by the law: infanticide. About thirty cases were dealt with by the Essex courts in the last forty years of the sixteenth century. Most involved illegitimate babies, and the usual way of disposing of them was by strangulation, smothering, or exposure to the cold. Very much later, in 1817, a mere ten women were charged in England and Wales with concealing births, although some cases of infant killings were presumably included in the general category of murder. There are two reasons for thinking that infanticide was in fact very much more common than the criminal records suggest. Firstly, in present-day underdeveloped communities with high birth rates, extreme poverty, and without the knowledge or techniques of contraception, there is usually a high incidence of abortion and infanticide. Secondly, inquiries made during the eighteenth century into the manner of caring for children by the Poor Law authorities in London and elsewhere clearly showed that there was a great wastage of young lives, some of which was deliberate.

During the eighteenth century the conditions of pauper children came to the attention of the public as the result of investigations by parliamentary committees and the work of philanthropists such as Thomas Coram and Jonas Hanway. Roughly speaking, a thousand babies under twelve months old and five or six hundred children aged between one year and ten years came into the care of the parish overseers in London every year, only about a dozen of whom could expect to survive to the age of ten. A major cause of the high mortality rate was the practice of placing children with parish nurses who frequently disposed of them. In 1715 a committee of the House of Commons investigated conditions in the parish of St Martin-in-the-Fields, reputed to be one of the most charitable in London, and found that three-quarters of babies born in the parish died each year and that

> A great many poor infants and exposed bastard children are inhumanely suffered to die by the barbarity of nurses, especially parish nurses, who are a sort of people void of commiseration or religion hired by the church-wardens to take off a burthen from the parish at the cheapest and easiest rates they can; and these know the

manner of doing it effectually, as by the burial books may evidently appear.[21]

According to Jonas Hanway, a dead child was

more pleasing and more familiar to the generality of common nurses than a living one; and that by habit they contract as little sensibility to the death of others as a common soldier after a dozen bloody campaigns.[22]

In 1739 Thomas Coram, with government backing, established in London the Foundling Hospital to 'prevent the frequent murders of poor miserable infants at their births' and to 'suppress the inhuman custom of exposing new-born infants to perish in the streets'. In the years 1741–50 it took in 1,384 children, 52 per cent of whom died; even so, the survival rate was much higher than among parish children. In 1756 the hospital yielded to government pressure and received admissions of infants from all parts of the country. From then until 1760 it received almost 15,000 infants, only one-third of whom lived to be apprentices at the age of ten. Most of the children taken in were very young indeed. During the first half of 1759, for example, 1,530 infants entering the hospital were under nineteen days old and another 741 were aged between five weeks and eleven months. Many babies were already sick when they arrived, and in these circumstances the survival rates achieved by the hospital were remarkably good. As far as was possible the hospital chose its nurses carefully, never placing more than three infants in the care of one nurse; and any nurse who lost as many as three babies was dismissed.

Meanwhile the huge losses among infants in the care of parishes continued. A survey carried out by Hanway of fourteen parishes in London between 1750 and 1755 showed that over 88 per cent of babies died in their care. In another parish in 1764 the mortality rate was 100 per cent. The reason was clear enough to Hanway:

Children were put into the hands of indigent, filthy, and decrepit women, three or four to one woman, and sometimes sleeping with them. The allowance of these women being scanty, they are tempted to take part of the bread and milk intended for the poor infants. The child cries for food and the nurse beats it because it cries. Thus with blows, starvings, and putrid air, with the addition of lice, itch and filthiness, he soon receives his quietus.

Hanway did not claim that the extremely high mortality found among parish children was caused entirely by deliberate action. Some would have died however they were cared for—witness the death rate among children looked after by the Foundling Hospital—and some died as the result of carelessness rather than malice. But Hanway continued:

Would not any man in his senses conclude, after the death of three or four children in one woman's hands, that the nurse was very unfortunate; and after five or six, that she was very ignorant or very wicked? But when in so short a period, the mortality of seven or eight had happened, would it not create a suspicion that she starved them or gave them sleeping potions? And would not the same common sense and candour lead one to think that, upon seeing the eighteenth child brought within this parish nurse's den, those who sent them preferred that they should die?[23]

Hanway wrote of London, where the problem was probably worse than in the provinces, for the overcrowding in the metropolis and hordes of casual labourers it attracted made it inevitable that there were large numbers of new-born pauper children, some of whom would be deliberately killed by parish nurses or, indeed, by their own parents. But there is no reason for believing that infanticide, or its euphemistic variant, 'overlaying', was exclusively a London sin. Indeed, during the period of the Foundling Hospital's existence, children were dispatched from provincial towns to London; not a few of them died on the way. Taken nationally, the disposal of unwanted infants had a cumulative effect on population history by removing potential mothers and fathers from the scene. In this sense infanticide was probably the most potent of all the forms of violent death.

Beyond the fatal effects of violence deliberately practised by man on man, there were the accidents of everyday life that took an unknown toll. Before the Industrial Revolution England had its quota of fatal industrial accidents, although there is no way of knowing whether they were proportionately more or less common than they are today. Some occupations were highly hazardous, including, for example, the shipping industry. On the admittedly unhealthy Africa run the Royal Africa Company lost half its captains between 1720 and 1724. But the life of common seamen, whether plying to the East Indies or risking the North Sea storms on a coastal collier, was always harsh and sometimes dangerous. 'No man will be a sailor who has contrivance enough to get himself into a jail,' remarked Dr Johnson, 'for being in a ship is being in a jail with the chance of being drowned. . . . A man in a jail has more room, better food, and commonly better company.'[24] In the later decades of the seventeenth century the merchant fleet employed roughly 50,000 men at any one time. A century later the fatality rate among men in the Royal Navy was six per thousand per year, counting only those drowned or killed in shipwrecks and fires on board ship, and a further thirty-two per thousand who died of disease or accident on board ship. If life in the merchant navy was equally hazardous in the late seventeenth century, then we have 300 men a year dying by drowning, shipwreck and fire, and another 1,600 perishing from disease or accident.

Another dangerous occupation was mining, where men

risked death from drowning, rock-falls, and explosion. The dangers increased as the coal-mining industry grew in importance and mines became deeper. As on so many subjects, John Aubrey had some information about accidents in coal mines:

> In the Bishoprick of Durham is a Coalery, which by reason of the dampes ther did so frequently kill the workmen (sometimes three or four in a Moneth). . . . It happened one time, that the workmen being merry with drink fell to play with fire-brands, and to throwe live-coales at one another at the head of the pitt, where they usually have fires. It fortuned that a fire-brand fell into the bottom of the Pitt: where at there proceeded such a noise as iff it had been a Gun: they likeing the sport, threw down more fire-brands and there followed the like noise, for severall times, and at length it ceased. They went to work after and were free from Damps, having by good chance found out this experiment, they do now every morning throw down some coales, and they work as securely as in any other mines.[25]

The registers of coal-mining parishes of the north of England have frequent references to the burials of men killed in mining accidents. But, in all, coal-mining employed no more than about 12,000 people in England at the end of the seventeenth century, so, however dangerous, it contributed relatively little to total mortality. Other forms of mining employed even fewer people and were probably less dangerous.

The most widespread occupation was, of course, farming, while in industry the manufacture of textiles or leather absorbed much more labour than shipping or mining. These were not in themselves dangerous occupations, although they were occasionally accompanied by fatal accident. An Essex milk-maid, on her way to attend her cows early one June morning in 1587, was savaged by two mastiffs and killed—not the fate normally thought to be awaiting milk-maids on a summer's morning. Probably the only slightly hazardous operation in textiles occurred in the finishing processes, where the dyers were sometimes overcome by the fumes from the vats. Leather manufacturers ran few risks, save perhaps for the chance of a tanner tumbling into the tan vat in a drunken stupor : the tan liquors gave off alcohol and the occasional swig helped the time pass by.

The weather added its own dangers to unwary travellers. Shortly before Christmas 1707 a butcher was found dead on the Derbyshire moors. He had been returning home from Ashbourne market when he was overcome by 'a most violent storm of wind and rain'. A double tragedy occurred in Derbyshire early in 1772, when two men returning from market were lost on the moors for two days before being found dead. But not only travellers were caught by the elements. A youth who stood under a tree at Dorking in Surrey about 1580 'scoffing at thunder' was 'stroke to death, his clothes stinking with a sulphurous stench'. Even more unfortunate was the wife of Richard Dickinson of Hackness in Yorkshire :

> Tewsday the Third of January [1659/60] was an exceeding stormie day and dyd drive snow verie fearsely and that day . . . shee being in the Chamber [of her house] there fell a greate drifte of shelfe of snowe from the hill and drave downe the House all but the Chimney and the next day shee was founde under the Thatch and snowe dead and their daughter and Child that were in yᵉ Chimney were saved alive and foure horses that were in the Stable were Laimed and Spoyled and dyed.[26]

Ultimately the picture that emerges of violent death is blurred and episodic. We know that pre-industrial society in England had a high tolerance of violence, and we may assume that in an agrarian-based, pre-mechanised society the hazards to life of storm and flood, darkness and 'acts of God' were high. What we do not know is how important such events were as causes of death compared with the toll taken by dearth and disease. If average mortality fluctuated around the thirty per thousand mark, how much of this was caused by war, riot and rebellion; how much by the violence of individuals against one another; and how much by the accidents accompanying work and pleasure? Not very much, we may guess. War, riot and rebellion rumbled away in a regular fashion, eroding a little of the male population in most years. But although war became more dangerous during the seventeenth and eighteenth centuries as armies became larger and generals discovered more efficient ways of killing the enemy, it took the nineteenth, and more particularly the twentieth, centuries to develop warfare as a means of annihilating vast populations. The legal system undoubtedly took a greater toll of human life before the nineteenth century than it did after 1800. But even during the eighteenth century the carnage of the gallows was dropping. In earlier centuries, perhaps, more Englishmen died of hanging than of hunger; but compared with griping of the guts, or famine fever, or poxes great and small, or bursting buboes, broken necks were not a danger that worried most men. As for accidental death, all life abounded with perils over which man had little control. At a time when death rates from natural causes were so high, the risks of falling off a horse or drowning in the sea were of little consequence.

F

# Grave Matters

'CHRISTIANS', wrote Sir Thomas Browne in 1658, 'have handsomely glossed the deformity of death, by careful consideration of the body, and civil rites which take off brutal terminations. And though they conceived all reparable by a resurrection, cast not off all care of enterrment.'[1] The reality of death produced a ritual designed to comfort the survivors, generated an industry to cater for the needs of the deceased and the mourners, and, in the large towns at least, posed a severe problem as the need of space for the dead competed with the need of space for the living. As for the survivors, the frequency of death shaped their lives no less than those of the departed. In pre-industrial England the family was both a social group and a unit of economic production. The death of a member reduced the claim on the family budget but also reduced the number of hands available for work. When a child died the economic balance might tilt to the benefit of the survivors, since the reduction in consumption was probably greater than the reduction of labour that occurred. If the father died, the eldest son might inherit and thus have the opportunity to marry and establish a family of his own. If the mother, then the household lacked cook and child-minder, and the widower might speedily remarry.

Preparations for death started on the sick-bed, if not before. For the prudent it was wise policy to make a will bequeathing property to heirs and successors and—very important—to make provision for a decent funeral in a style suited to one's station in life. However, to judge from the frequency of such phrases as 'sick in body but sound in mind' found at the beginning of wills, it seems that many people postponed the drawing up of a will until death stared them in the face. As well as the earthly arrangements, there was the business of making one's peace with God. Again, the prudent attended to this before the onset of sickness. William Blundell wrote in the late seventeenth century:

> While I am in health I may do well to make and write down a prayer, protestation, or soliloquy, just such a one as I would desire to say in the extremity of my last sickness. By this I may renounce all thoughts, words, and deeds contrary to a good Christian, which shall happen, or to which I shall be tempted at the time. I may beg of God to assist my soul while my body lies in torment, and by the extreme anguish thereof, hath stupefied or perverted my reason. I beg likewise grace for my friends that stand by to assist me, that they may not be scandalised either at the rage or stupidity which may happen unto me by the force of the sickness. And I may offer myself up to suffer more and longer torments if it be God's pleasure I should do so; and that grace may be allowed to bear them, I may carry this paper about me, to the end that it may be read to me in my sickness.[2]

The wisdom of Blundell's precautions had been tragically underlined by the manner of the passing of Robert Cecil, Earl of Salisbury, in 1612. Salisbury was then perhaps the richest and certainly the most powerful man in England, yet neither his wealth nor his power could buy a peaceful end. He first became ill in 1609 and from then on fell intermittently into the hands of doctors, apothecaries and surgeons who bled, dosed and purged him with considerable enthusiasm, greater expense, but no beneficial results. By the spring of 1612 he was desperately ill and, with swollen legs and a body covered in sores, he was carried on pillows of down in a specially prepared litter from London to Bath where, it was hoped, the waters might do some good. By now his chaplain was in attendance, for it was clear that the physicians had done their worst. Perhaps remembering the great wealth he had amassed, sometimes by dubious means, during his lifetime, Salisbury prayed: 'My audit is made, Let me come now, O Jesus, in the strength of my understanding, in the act of my memory.' The sick man eventually died at Marlborough on his way back to London. Reviewing the episode, the historian of the Cecils, Professor Stone, has speculated that a traitor's death on the block, which could conceivably have befallen Salisbury had the power struggle with Essex at the end of the sixteenth century concluded differently, would have been preferable to being, in the words of the playwright John Ford, tumbled 'from bed to bed, be massacred alive by some physicians, for a month or two, in hope of freedom from a fever's torment'.[3]

When death came at last, the scene was set for the funeral. 'Man is a Noble Animal, splendid in ashes, and pompous in the grave.'[4] It was important for all ranks of society that funerals should be in keeping with the lifestyle of the deceased. In essentials the stages of a funeral were much the same for rich and poor alike: the preparations, the interment, and the entertainments and mourning afterwards. But these simple ingredients were overlaid with ceremonial, pomp and display according to the wealth of the deceased and his standing in the community. Local customs also adorned Christian burials with symbolic acts of sometimes doubtful religious significance and origin.

The first task was to send for someone to prepare the body. As a result of the plague epidemics that afflicted seventeenth-century London it was obligatory not only to inform the minister of the parish when the death took place, but also to call in 'searchers' appointed by the city authorities to inspect the body for signs of contagious disease. Among the middle and upper classes it was a fairly common practice to embalm the body. This was made necessary by the length of time that often elapsed between death and burial, an interval during which relations and friends were summoned and preparations made for the funeral. As with so many other aspects of funerals, the cost and elaboration of embalming varied with the status of the recipient: five shillings was sufficient for a minor gentleman in 1580, but £20 was required for a more substantial knight nearly a century later. Embalming may have fallen a little out of fashion in some circles in the early seventeenth century, but it was still common enough among the well-to-do a century later. One gentleman dying in 1691 willed fifty guineas to his doctors and apothecaries for embalming him, and another fifty for his coffin.

Coffins were optional extras, although they became more usual, even among the lower ranks, during the eighteenth century. In the Derbyshire parish of Bakewell, for example, the parish register noted that 'the custom of Interment in Wooden coffins . . . was on the Rev^d Mr Monks coming to reside here' (i.e. in 1678). The same source noted as late as 1797: 'A corps from Sheldon was brought in swandling clothes . . . and was detained in Church until a coffin was made, and the wife then took off the flannel for her own use.' In one Sussex parish in 1608 the body of a poor man was brought to church 'half naked with his face bare, [and] the parson would not bury him soe, but first he gave a sheete and caused him to be sacked therein, and they buried him more Christian like, being much grieved to see him brought soe unto the grave'. Non-coffined burials were cheaper in two ways: not only were the deceased's survivors saved the cost of a coffin, but burial fees were lower as well. At Birchington, Kent, it cost 8d. to inter a 'coffin'd person', but only 6d.

for a 'noe coffin'd person'.⁵ Similar differentials applied elsewhere. In some parishes open coffins were supplied into which the corpse was placed during the recital of the burial service; after the service the body was removed and lowered into the ground with strips of canvas.

Coffined or not, the dead were usually arranged in funeral clothes for their final earthly journey. In the early eighteenth century the French traveller H. Misson provided a lengthy account of English funeral practices among 'middling People, among whom the Customs of a Nation are most truly to be learn'd'. The corpses of men were washed and shaved and dressed in a long white shirt or shift, which 'may be had ready made, of what Size or Price you please, for People of every Age and Sex'. The shift was fastened at the wrists and front with laces, and also at the foot, where it was turned up at the end to form a kind of bag. A cap was placed on the head and tied around the chin, gloves put on the hands, and a cravat about the neck. Women were similarly attired, except for a head-dress in place of the cap. Then, 'that the Body may ly the softer, some put a lay of Bran, about four Inches thick, at the Bottom of the Coffin'.⁶ This was an old practice. In the early seventeenth century, for example, the Duchess of Richmond ordered in her will that she should not be embalmed—'for soe my sweete Lord out of his tender love commanded me that I should not be opened'—but 'be presentlie be putt up in brann and in lead before I am fully could'.⁷

It did not escape the eyes either of commercially-minded men or of the government that large quantities of cloth were every year buried in the ground; and it seemed a good idea, at times when England's woollen trade was depressed, to ensure that all shrouds should be made of woollen cloth. As early as 1622, during a period of acute depression in the woollen cloth industry, the Privy Council had proclaimed that mourning clothes should be made 'only of Cloth and Stuffes, made of the Wooll of this

Kingdome, and not elsewhere, nor otherwise'.[8] In 1666, and more effectively again in 1678, acts of parliament obliged the use of woollen shrouds. As part of the process of enforcement, relatives had to produce affidavits that the body had been properly attired, and many parishes kept special books in which to record such burials. Thus the rector of St John's Church, Peterborough, entered in the parish register: 'The act for burying in woollen taking place August ye first, 1678, Xtianings and Marriages are only registered in this book, and burials in ye New Booke provided for ye purpose.' The entries were usually matter-of-fact, such as at Littleborne in Kent, where the vicar recorded, inter alia, 'Jane Hawkins Widow was buried according to ye said Act on ye seventh day of November, Affidavit was brought in on ye 10th day of ye same Month.' But at least one rector in Northamptonshire seems to have regarded the law as an ass in the 1680s and made his feelings known in the parish register:

> 1680, June 16. Thomas Shortland, the son of Thomas Shortland of the Parish of Helmdon, being Dead was put into a pithole and Bury'd in the churchyard of the Town above written. Memorandum That within the revolution of eight days after the Funerall obsequays of Thos Shortland Affidavit was brought from a justice of the Peace that the said Thomas Shortland was well wrapped in a shirt of wollen and was let down into his dormitory with that vestment about his corps to the great satisfaction of a Law enjoineing that Habiliment as convenient for the Dead.[9]

Not everyone relished the idea of rotting away in wool. As Alexander Pope wrote in *Moral Essays*:

'Odious!' in woollen! 'twould a saint provoke,'
Were the last words that poor Narcissa spoke.

In January 1703

The Right Hon^ble Henry Jermyn was buried in ye south side of ye church [at Rushbrooke in Suffolk]. Because he was buried in Linnen contrary to an Act for burying in woollen only, therefore by order from a warrant from a Justice of the Peace fifty shillings was paid to the Informer and fifty shillings to the Poor of the Parish upon the Sunday next following.[10]

In common with other legislation of the time, the enforcement of the acts obliging the use of woollen shrouds was left to informers who split the penalty with the parish where the offence took place.

Once the corpse had been made ready, the stage was set for the funeral. This was elaborate or simple according to the lifestyle of the principal participant. Misson described the practice found in the middle ranks of society in the early eighteenth century:

They send the Beadle with a List of such Friends and Relations as they have a mind to invite; and sometimes they have printed Tickets, which they leave at their houses. A little before the company is set in Order for the March, they lay the body into a Coffin upon two stools, in a Room, where all that please may go and see it. . . . Upon this Occasion, the rich Equipage of the Dead does Honour to the Living. The Relations and Chief Mourners are in a Chamber apart, with their most intimate Friends; and the rest of the Guests are dispersed in several Rooms about the House. When they are ready to set out they nail up the coffin, and a Servant presents the Company with sprigs of Rosemary: Everyone takes a Sprig and carries it in his hand 'till the Body is put into the Grave, at which time they all throw their Sprigs in after it.[11]

The pall-bearers were accoutred in black mourning crepe, and crepe and ribbon were also distributed to the family servants of wealthy people and to the poor who followed

the corpse to the grave. Taking into account the black
drapes used to adorn the house of the deceased, the hearse
and the church, the demands on the cloth industry were
very considerable. In the sixteenth century funerals of the
aristocracy could consume between 500 and 1,200 yards
of black cloth; the particularly sumptuous funeral of the
Earl of Northumberland in 1489 used over 2,200 yards
of cloth. The cost could sometimes be reduced by hiring
drapes from the parish, which might keep a supply for
the purpose. According to Misson, the 'parish has always
three or four Mortuary Cloths of different prices. . . . The
handsomest is hir'd out at five or six crowns.'[12] Although
costs and consumption could thereby be cut, the volume
of cloth used by the funeral industry was still very large.
During the reign of Queen Anne the frequent death of
her many relations threw the drapery trade into turmoil.
The Court was perpetually going into black, and Court
ladies were emulated by many other women not connected with the Court but who nevertheless attired themselves in mourning in the hope that their neighbours would
think they were. Mercers found it difficult to supply the
demand for black ribbons and equally difficult to dispose
of their stocks of coloured cloths. In the eighteenth century
some parts of the textile industry, particularly in Essex,
specialised in the production of bunting and flags for the
navy and mourning crepes for funerals, and in 1772
Arthur Young described Sudbury as a town containing
'a great number of hands, who earn their livelihood by
working up the wool from the sheeps back to the weaving
it into says and burying crepes'.[13]

Funeral processions were arranged with great elaboration. A particularly splendid occasion was the funeral in
1572 of the Earl of Derby, who was accompanied on
the two-mile journey from his home to the church by
eight hundred people, including family mourners, local
gentry, servants, heralds, clergy, choristers, and one
hundred poor men dressed in black. This style of depart-

G

ure became a little less lavish at the end of the sixteenth
century. Nevertheless, the ritual of the procession
remained common. According to John Aubrey, the number of people in the procession equalled the age in years
of the deceased, but this was not always so. Following the
death of William Harvey in June 1657 the Fellows of the
Royal College of Physicians were 'reminded that they
attend the solemnities of Dr Harvey's funeral to be held
next day, in their gowns'.[14] Accordingly a gaggle of rather
elderly gentlemen followed the body 'lapt in lead', on a
ponderous journey from London to the village of Hemp-
stead on the Essex-Suffolk border. There he was laid to
rest in the family vault. One of the bearers was John
Aubrey, a close friend. 'I was at his Funerall, and helpt
to carry him into the Vault.'[15]

It is clear from such descriptions that the corpse was
commonly accompanied to the grave by kinsmen—
although not necessarily by more distant relations—
friends and neighbours, servants and dependants, if any,
and social peers. Thus the body of Sir William Fitzwilliam,
a wealthy Merchant Taylor of London and Merchant of
the Staple of Calais, was escorted out of London in 1534
by members of the companies of Merchant Taylors and
Staplers on the first stage of its journey to Northamptonshire, where Sir William had established himself as a
country gentleman by buying land with his mercantile
wealth. Two centuries later the body of the third Earl of
Cardigan was carried from Wiltshire, where he died,
into his home county of Northamptonshire, where the
cortège was met by the local gentry; six of them, two
knights and four esquires, carried the pall to the family
vault in Dene church.

It was sometimes the custom for unmarried girls who
died to be carried to the grave only by women, although
men might be present in the early stages of the funeral.
For example, the little daughter of the Rev. Ralph
Josselin was borne to her grave in 1650 by four women,

friends of the family and relations, though at the outset the coffin had been accompanied by 'most of the Towne'. Two years earlier the Josselins had buried an infant son, and in his case, too, 'the gravest matrons in the towne layde his tombe into the earth'.[16] According to Misson, 'no Men ever go to Women's Burials, nor the Women to the Men's', although the women did attend the accompanying festivities where they 'will hold it out with the Men, when they have a Bottle before them . . . and tattle infinitely better than they'.[17] But this ungallant Frenchman was not always an accurate observer, and there is plenty of evidence of mixed funerals in England as well as of mixed drinking.

The wealthy and socially distinguished were buried in the parish church or perhaps in a family vault, while others found their final resting place in the churchyard. The choice of church or churchyard was again largely a matter of social status. To the mind of the father-in-law of the diarist John Evelyn, churches were becoming cluttered with the corpses of social upstarts in the late seventeenth century and he instructed in his will that

> his body should be buried in the churchyard under the south-east window óf the chancel adjoining to the burial places of his ancestors . . . he being much offended by the novel custom of burying everyone within the body of the church and chancel, that being a great favour heretofore granted to the martyrs and great persons, this excess of making churches charnel-houses being of ill and irreverent example and prejudicial to the health of the living, besides the continual disturbance of the pavement and seats, and several other indecencies.[18]

At about the same time the Bishop of London commented: 'The churchyard for the dead, the church for the living.'

In the country parishes the churchyards were able to

cope comfortably enough with the ever-multiplying community of corpses into the nineteenth and twentieth centuries, but the cities, and London in particular, were running out of space by the eighteenth century, and sometimes long before. According to John Stow, the historian of London, writing in 1598, the Black Death of 1348 caused a burial crisis, for 'churchyards were not sufficient to receive the dead, but men were forced to choose out certain fields for burial'; in both 1348 and the following year additional areas of land were bought in the suburbs and consecrated as burial grounds. Stow also reported that in 1549 a chapel and charnel-house belonging to the parish of St Faith's, lying close to St Paul's Cathedral, were converted into dwelling-houses, warehouses and sheds; the bones from the charnel-house were taken by the cartload to Finsbury, where they were 'laid on a moorish ground, in short space after raised, by soilage of the city upon them, to bear three windmills'.[19] In the eighteenth century the congested state of the churchyards posed a serious threat to public health, and many parishes had to look for additional land to bury the dead. For example, in February 1747 the parish of St Andrew in Holborn proposed to buy extra land, since the population of the parish had doubled during the preceding forty years and the existing churchyards

> are so full of Corps, that it is difficult to dig a Grave without digging up some Parts of a Corps before decayed; which makes it very offensive to the Inhabitants, and the Reason many Corps are carried out of the Parish to be buried.[20]

During the nineteenth century the pressure on burial space in the large cities was eased only by the creation of private enterprise cemetery companies.

At the church or graveside the coffin was met by the clergyman, who conducted the burial service. Funeral sermons were a customary feature of the ceremony. In

April 1657 the Rev. Ralph Josselin preached a sermon that 'continued till sundown' at the burial service of a neighbouring gentlewoman, during which he lost his 'greife and trouble much in the pulpitt'.[21] Misson noted that 'Either a Funeral-Sermon is preach'd, containing an Elogium upon the deceased, or certain Prayers said, adapted to the Occasion.'[22]

The ceremonies over, the mourners and guests returned home for the concluding festivities: 'They return home in the same Order that they came, and each drinks two or three glasses more before he goes home,' reported Misson, describing a 'middling' style of funeral. But the level of hospitality could be more generous, especially among the aristocratic. As many as 1,900 people were feasted at the funeral of the Duke of Norfolk in 1524, and 3,000 or 4,000 poor people were fed from the left-overs of the funeral feast of the Earl of Rutland in 1587. In addition, gifts of gloves and scarves were given to the servants of the deceased and perhaps to other people as well. At the funeral of Sir Richard Piggott in 1685 'the Gentry had Rings, all the servants gloves. We had burnt wine and biscuits in great plenty.'[23] At the more modest levels of society inhabited by Josselin, he himself once sent six dozen cakes to a funeral feast; on another occasion he disparagingly commented that 'Not a glove, ribband, scutcheon, wine, beare, bisquett were given [at the funeral of Lady Honeywood] . . . but a little mourning to servants.'[24] Such an omission was unusual. Even among the poor, entertainment was generally provided after a funeral, often at a level well beyond their resources: death, like Christmas and harvest time, provided an excuse for eating and drinking in a style out of keeping with ordinary life.

For a variety of reasons some funerals took place at night. One was economy. John Weaver, writing in 1631, explained that

Funerals in any expensive way here with us are now accounted but a fruitlesse vanitie, insomuch that almost all the ceremoniall rites of obsequies heretofore used are altogether laid aside; for wee see daily that noblemen and gentlemen of emminent ranks, office and qualitie are either silentlie buried in the night time, with a torch, a two-penie linke, and a lanterne; or parsimoniously interred in the day-time by the helpe of some ignorant countray-painter, without the attendance of any one of the officers of armes.[25]

But nocturnal burials were also given on occasions as a mark of honour. Until the early seventeenth century former Lords Mayor of London were ceremonially buried by torchlight, and in several parts of the country local gentry were by custom laid finally to rest by night. Thus in June 1668 Viscount Fitzharding was buried at Bruton in Somerset 'between twelve and one of the clock in the night, after a sermon preached by Mr John Randall . . . buried in a vault in the Chancell in a coffin of leadd'. By 1737 the practice of nocturnal burials had grown to such an extent in Wellingborough, Northamptonshire, that it had become 'a very inconvenient and prejudicial custom both to the minister and inhabitants'.[26] The parish therefore ordered that funerals should take place no later than 7 p.m. in the summer and 4 p.m. in the winter.

There were also less honourable reasons for burial by night. In August 1659 at Alstonfield in Staffordshire the body of Humphrey Dakin was 'buried about two of the clock in the night, fearing an arrest'. This arose from the bizarre practice whereby creditors could arrest a corpse for debt, although it is not clear what was to be done with the prize once it had been acquired. This problem was apparently never resolved in the case of John Matthews, whose corpse 'was stopt on the churchway for debt' in the Buckinghamshire village of Sparsholt in

August 1689. 'And having laine there fower days, was by justices warrant buryed in the place to prevent annoyances—but about six weeks after it was by an Order of Sessions taken up and buried in the Churchyard by the wife of the deceased.' As well as debtors, suicides were also candidates for night interments. These unfortunates often finished up, not in the churchyard at all, but buried at the crossroads with a stake driven through the body. Thus in Derbyshire in 1573 'Thos Maule fd hunge on a tree by ye wayeside after a druncken fitte . . . [was] at midd nighte burried at ye highest crosse roades wt a stake yn hym.'[27] As an act of grace local rectors sometimes permitted suicides to be interred in the churchyard without ceremonial, and an act of 1821 ordered that they be buried in churchyards between the hours of 9 and 12 p.m.

After the funeral there remained the task of erecting a suitable memorial. John Aubrey left instructions for his own tombstone: 'I would desire that this Inscription should be a stone about the bigness of a royal sheet of paper, scilicet, about 2 foot square. Mr Reynolds of Lambeth, Stonecutter . . . will help me to a Marble as square as an imperial sheet of paper for 8 shillings.' His request was not carried out and his only memorial was an entry in the parish register of the church of St Mary Magdalene, Oxford, where he was buried: '1697, JOHN AUBERY A Stranger was buryed June 7th.'[28] Such neglect was untypical: all but the poorest usually had their last resting place marked by a cross, stone, or a more elaborate construction.

As with other aspects of funerals, monuments were largely a matter of rank: 'Sepulchres should be made according to the quality and degree of the persons deceased, that by the tomb everyone might be discerned of what rank he was living,' thought one authority writing in 1631. But fashion also played a part. During the reign of Elizabeth a nobleman was apt to be laid to rest under a great figured tomb 'breathtaking in its arrogance'.

Professor Stone has pointed out that many of the tombs erected to honour Elizabethan and Jacobean noblemen were 'some of the largest and heaviest monuments to private individuals that England had seen since the days of the round barrow'.[29] From about the 1620s, however, considerations both of taste and expense moved in the direction of smaller, less ostentatious memorials. The details of tombs also changed over time. Medieval carvers rarely tried to provide a portrait of the subject on the memorials they made, but carved instead a representative lady or gentleman appropriate to the status and sex of the deceased. This figure was frequently surrounded by saints, angels and 'weepers'. After the Reformation, the weepers remained but the saints and angels disappeared and were replaced by cadavers, skulls, crossbones, urns, lamps and allegorical figures derived from the revived interest in classical antiquity.

The manufacture of tombs and memorials was a busy industry. Aubrey was behaving with uncharacteristic modesty when thinking of a piece of marble for his own tomb costing only eight shillings. At the peak of aristocratic extravagance at the turn of the sixteenth and seventeenth centuries an elaborate memorial might cost anything between £500 and £1,000; more modest figured tombs for gentlemen probably started at around £50 in the 1630s but could easily rise to three figures. The sepulchral ambitions of the English nobility, county gentlemen, prosperous merchants and professional families, to say nothing of the more simple requirements of yeomen and tenant farmers, generated a large expenditure and created employment for monumental masons. According to a correspondent of Hogarth writing in 1755, 'sculpture in England has hitherto been almost wholly monumental'.[30] Until the sixteenth century sculptors were generally local men using local supplies of alabaster and stone, but during the sixteenth century the industry tended to concentrate in London, where masons would execute orders to more or less standardised designs for supplying to all parts of the country. For example, the memorial stone to William Harvey, consisting of a life-sized bust in white marble, a coat of arms, and a Latin inscription, was made by a London stonemason. It is noticeable that Aubrey, who expected to be buried in Wiltshire but was in fact buried in Oxford, arranged for his memorial tablet to be made by a stonecutter in Lambeth; perhaps it was the logistic difficulties created by this arrangement that resulted in his ending up in an unmarked grave. However, local monumental masons by no means disappeared, for the demand was sufficiently large to support both a London-based national trade and local craftsmen. Thus at Burton-on-Trent, where there were good supplies of alabaster, a father and son were at work in the 1570s 'turning out dozens of effigies of the most conventional order, the tomb chests adorned with Italian detail grossly misunderstood, misrepresented, and copied with supreme unintelligence, mistakes and all, from tomb to tomb'.[31]

The expenditure on memorials was only part of the total cost of dying which could, on occasions, rise to very high levels. Tudor noblemen not infrequently encumbered their estates with costs of over £1,000, and occasionally over £2,000 or £3,000, at their dying, although there are signs that the peak of expenditure came in the 1580s and that thereafter a period of retrenchment set in. As the second Earl of Dorset explained in 1608, expensive funerals were 'only good for the heraldes and drapers and very prejudiciall to the children, servantes and friendes of the deceased'.[32] Even so, the requirements of rank set limits to the extent to which economy could go. 'And as touching my funeralles,' wrote a Yorkshire knight in 1568, 'I will my executors shall make preparacion for suche necessarye thinges to be used at that tyme as shal be seamelie and decente for my degree and callinge.'[33] For the wealthier country gentry a 'seamelie and decente' burial might cost anything between £50 and £200 in the late sixteenth and early seventeenth century, plus, of course, the cost of a suitable memorial. The lesser gentry, by cutting expenditure to the bone, might be interred for as little as £5 or £10.

At that level of expenditure, a gentleman's style of burial was dropping below that of a yeoman. For example, in 1583 the funeral of a substantial Oxfordshire yeoman cost less than £4. Half of this was 'geeven to the poore in bread'; the rest was for digging the grave, payments 'to the Ringers, to Ring all the belles in the Day of his Buriall', and for sundry other expenses. But this was excessively modest. Elizabethan and Stuart yeomen often bequeathed considerable sums of money, perhaps exceeding £20 or £30, to be spent on entertaining their neighbours and the poor on the occasion of their burial. Even among that stratum of society, unable to boast of any elevated social status, it was deemed proper to provide for a decent burial. Thus in 1703 the executors of Robert Stubbs, a modest shoemaker of Penrith, spent £2 13s. 8d. on his funeral out of a total estate worth less than £36. During the eighteenth century the friendly societies and box clubs established among artisans in London and elsewhere spent a good deal of their funds on funerals. According to Patrick Colquhoun, writing at the beginning of the nineteenth century, such money would have been better spent on the survivors, but 'there is a disposition among all the lower classes of the people to have what is called a decent funeral and this frequently amounts to from ten to fifteen pounds'.[34]

Remembering the general level of poverty in pre-industrial England, it may seem that an excessively large amount of resources was devoted to burying and commemorating the dead. Whether such an expenditure was justified can be considered only in relation to ideas of the time. At the material level, the entertainment lavished at funerals was a respite from the pinched diets of every-day life: death, like birth, marriage and ecclesiastical festivals, provided an opportunity for voracious eating, made no less enjoyable by being at somebody else's expense. It is noticeable how the poor were often specifically included in the hospitality provided at the funerals of the gentry and yeomanry. The death of the head of a family might be followed by the breaking-up of the household and the dismissal of personal servants; on these occasions the funeral feast might have the additional flavour of a farewell dinner.

But the food and gifts dispensed at funerals had a deeper significance. They were a token of status, a symbol of the position occupied by the deceased in his local community. A Lancashire yeoman wrote in his will at the end of the sixteenth century: 'And I doe give sixe poundes in mony to be bestowed in a dinner to make my honest neighbours welcome for my last faire well to them.'[35] Before the nineteenth century England consisted of many local communities that were largely self-contained, and the social position of individuals was determined largely by how their neighbours regarded them. An essential part of this regard was the level of hospitality that was dispensed both in life and in death. Friends and neighbours expected entertainment appropriate to the style of the deceased, while those who prized their position in the local community accepted that they should offer an appropriate level of hospitality even in death. Similar ideas were responsible for the display of memorial tablets and tombs: the community expected them to be on a scale in keeping with the rank occupied by the person who was commemorated. They were symbols that had meaning, less in terms of their artistic qualities or even of their religious significance, but more in terms of the prevailing concepts of society and status.

Funerals, feasts and memorials were also important aspects of the whole paraphernalia of mourning. When her brother died in 1690, Molly Verney wrote to her grandfather, who was concerned about money: 'I believe

you would have me mourn handsomely for so dear a
brother, and since there is none left but myself to mourn
for him, and I beg that I may have a tippet bought me,
since every gentlewoman has one as makes any show in
the world, it will cost £5 at least.'[36]

The frequency of death in pre-industrial England led
to a resigned acceptance of it. Nevertheless, grief still
needed to be assuaged. In *The Winter's Tale* Leontes, on
hearing of the death of his son and his wife, and suspect-
ing that his baby daughter also was dead, was told by
Paulina: 'What's gone and what's past help should be
past grief.'[37] He nevertheless nurtured his grief for sixteen
years—or perhaps it was remorse, for he had been per-
sonally responsible for the high casualty rate among his
relations. The Rev. Ralph Josselin, who died in 1683, saw
five of his ten children die, including two in infancy and
one in childhood. His most obvious emotion was resignation, although he was deeply moved by the death of
his eight-year-old Mary: 'Shee was a child of ten thousand, full of wisdome, womanlike gravity, knowledge,
sweet expressions of God, apt in her learning. . . . Lord I
rejoyce I had such a present for thee. . . . It lived desired
and dyed lamented, thy memory is and will bee sweete
unto mee.'[38]

Resignation, and a certain macabre detachment, is also
expressed in the following seventeenth-century epitaph:

Christopher Michell's Sonn Lyeth here, Richard
   Michell was his Name,
His Father's love was so to him, he caus'd to write the
   same:
He was but 4 Yeares 5 Moneths old, and then was
   buryed here,
And of his Body the wormes did find a Dish of dainty
   chere.[39]

Resignation and grief were likewise mingled in the mind
of John Evelyn when his five-year-old son Richard and

his baby son George died within three weeks of one another in 1658. 'I go even mourning to the grave,' he wrote in his diary.[40] Neither the familiarity of death nor the Christian comfort of the life hereafter lessened the mourning of men for their loved ones; and their expenditure on funerals and memorials helped to soften the loss.

The living buried their dead, commemorated them in feasts and tombstones, mourned them, and went on with the business of living. The frequency of death in England before the nineteenth century had profound effects on social and economic life. It was commonplace for parents to witness the deaths of several of their children and, conversely, for children to be left fatherless or motherless by the time they had reached adolescence. As far as the family was concerned, high mortality affected it both as a unit of production and as a unit of consumption. In the former case, much depended on the age-groups most affected by heavy mortality. The death of infants or very old people made little difference to the ability of the family farm or the family business to function efficiently; indeed, there might be a benefit, since less of the family's resources would go on consumption. But if the older children and young adults died, then the loss of manpower could be serious. One manifestation of this problem was the speed with which many widowers remarried, often within months of the death of their former partners. No doubt the desire for a warm bed was part of the explanation of the rush to the altar, but there were also acute practical difficulties in a household containing young children without a woman to look after them and attend to the running of the home. At a national level, the loss of manpower occasioned by high mortality was part of the interlocking problems of low productivity, low incomes, poor living conditions and high mortality. The deaths of young people about to enter the most productive period of their lives, and of able-bodied adults trained by experience or apprenticeship, represented a waste of economic resources that bore heavily on an impoverished economy.

The household was also a unit of consumption. The more that households consumed, the smaller were the surpluses of production or income available for trade and investment. Recent studies have shown that the average number of persons in an English household (including servants) was a little under five from the sixteenth to the nineteenth centuries, compared with just over three for England and Wales in the 1960s. Furthermore, households were typically composed of parents and younger children, of whom there were rarely more than two or three. This was partly because children tended to leave home at adolescence to become apprentices or servants, and because young adults, when marrying, established households of their own. But high levels of mortality, especially among babies and children, also operated to keep families relatively small. Thus high mortality tended to ease the pressures on consumption, except in so far that the rituals accompanying death and burial required relatively heavy outlays.

In the second half of the eighteenth century the population of England moved into a new era that has lasted to the present day, during which both the numbers of people in the country and their standard of living have risen. Over the two centuries from 1500 to 1700 the population of England and Wales did little more than double; during the next two centuries the population increased more than fivefold. The mechanics of this increase in its later stages, from about the middle of the nineteenth century, are fairly clear. Death rates, after being fairly stable at around twenty-one or twenty-two per thousand from the 1840s to the 1870s, declined to sixteen per thousand by the early twentieth century and twelve per thousand by the Second World War. Meanwhile the birth rate remained in the thirties per thousand until the 1890s

and then fell sharply, but always stayed above the death
rate. Behind these vital statistics were advances in medical
science and improvements in the material environment
brought about by industrialisation. There was a vast
saving of lives, especially of babies and young children.
As far as fertility was concerned, a growing knowledge
and practice of contraception and changing social
attitudes reduced the birth rate. But what happened
during the century or so before 1840? Did the harvest of
death diminish, or was the growth of population the
product of rising fertility?

The demographic revolution of the later eighteenth and
early nineteenth centuries is still a matter of great con-
troversy in spite of several generations of historical investi-
gation. The major source of uncertainty is that up to 1837
demographers have to work from estimates of fertility
and mortality which are subject to considerable margins
of error. The possibility of error becomes particularly
great precisely at the time when it is most crucial, that is
in the later eighteenth century. It was in this period, when
the demographic revolution was getting under way, that
the parish registration of baptisms and burials, on which
estimates of birth and death rates are based, becomes
unreliable, simply because population was growing at an
accelerating rate in regions where the organisation of
Anglican parishes was weak. The best estimates suggest
that crude birth rates rose somewhat during the eighteenth century, particularly in industrialised districts,
where there was a strong demand for labour to encourage
early marriages. The trend of the death rate is uncertain,
although it was probably a few points lower at the end of
the eighteenth century than at the beginning. However,
by 1800 it was probably still in the high twenties per
thousand. In the 1840s, when civil registration statistics
are available, the death rate was in the low twenties.

Thus pre-industrial levels of mortality seem to have
been reduced in two stages: a slight downward trend

during the eighteenth century, and a more substantial fall in the early nineteenth century. But more significant than the slight fall in the 'normal' death rate in the eighteenth century was the flattening-out of the violent oscillations of mortality characteristic of earlier periods. What, then, was happening to those forces that had traditionally kept mortality so high? Were advances in medicine and public health at last offering effective defences against disease? Were people becoming better fed, better housed, and better clothed, and so more resistant to sickness? Or were diseases themselves becoming less deadly?

It is impossible to make a positive assessment of the contribution made by medical progress in reducing the death rate during the eighteenth century. On the whole it does not appear that medicine was a particularly significant factor. We have seen that inoculation helped to reduce mortality from smallpox, but it has yet to be proved that it made a major contribution to the defeat of the disease. An older generation of historians thought that the increase in the number of provincial hospitals during the eighteenth century reduced the death rate, although it was later argued that hospitals were centres for the collection of the dying rather than for the cure of the living. The work of eighteenth-century hospitals has recently been seen in a more favourable light, and they have been shown to have had a low death rate and a high 'cure' rate. But their part in reducing total mortality can only have been small. They tended not to admit incurable cases, and they refused to accept infectious patients. Hospitals were also few in number in relation to the total population. There were about fifty new hospitals established by 1800; at best, they saved some lives in provincial towns but had little effect in the country districts.

Other medical advances, such as the use of mercury or quinine, had limited effects, and although medical knowledge was being extended during the eighteenth century, medical practice lagged well behind. Turning to public health, municipalities were no better equipped in the eighteenth century than they had been earlier. No doubt efforts to keep the streets clean and the water supplies pure helped to combat infection, but with the growth of urban population after 1750, local authorities found themselves with an uphill battle on their hands. Indeed, by the 1820s or 1830s there were signs that the battle was being lost in some of the most rapidly growing industrial cities and that death rates were temporarily rising again, although not to pre-industrial heights.

If medicine and public health offer no convincing explanation for the fall in mortality, what of economic improvement? In the long run the industrialisation of Britain after 1750 brought substantial material benefits to the population. But the position before 1800 is ambiguous. There were definite advances in agricultural methods and increases in agricultural output; there was the beginning of a revolution in industrial methods and organisation, and a revolution in transport based on rivers and canals. Total national income was rising, but so too was population. Probably there was a modest increase in output per head of population, although not all of this was available for additional personal consumption. Some of the extra income went on financing the investment required to make the expansion of output possible; and, by the 1790s, rising government expenditure on war took incomes away from personal consumers. Thus in the half century or so before 1800 there is no overwhelming case for believing that the mass of the population was living in markedly better conditions than had been the case in the first half of the eighteenth century. Food supplies were probably a little more regular, at least until the sequence of bad harvests at the very end of the century, and new crops such as the potato provided a valuable supplement to the traditional grain diets. Better transport and improved means of distribution may have contributed to the elimination of local food shortages. The products of the rapidly growing cotton industry, cheaper soap, pottery and ironware, all helped to create healthier living conditions. But by themselves they do not seem capable of explaining all of the decline in mortality during the eighteenth century.

This decline, it will be remembered, was of two kinds: a slight fall in the 'normal' death rate; and a flattening of those disastrous peaks of mortality when normal rates doubled or trebled. These disappeared in the 1740s and did not return. Was their disappearance connected with improving economic conditions, or was it the result of changes in the nature of major epidemic disease, or growing immunity? Plague had already vanished from England of its own accord before 1700. Dysentery, too, apparently declined in virulence during the eighteenth century, despite the growth of urban populations which increased the problems of sanitation and water supplies. Typhus became a less serious killer, perhaps because improvements in food supplies resulted in a better-fed population, but more likely because the population was becoming immune. Smallpox became a less dangerous disease, whether through inoculation or through a natural change in the disease itself is arguable.

We have, then, the possibility that mortality fell initially because the major epidemics relaxed their grip on the community for reasons that had nothing to do with either medicine or improving economic conditions. That they did not effectively return after 1750 may be due to the changing material environment in the later eighteenth century. A better-fed, better-clothed and better-housed population was probably more resistant to those devastating diseases that had kept mortality so high in pre-industrial England.

# Notes

Notes have been used to identify the sources of quotations. Here only the author's name is given, followed by the volume number, if appropriate, and the page number. Full bibliographical details are given in the bibliography. Where more than one work by an author appears in the bibliography, the relevant one may be identified by the date of the preferred edition.

CHAPTER 1 (pp. 1–14).
1. Quoted in Keynes, 224.  2. Quoted in Haggard, 28.
3. Eaton, 117.  4. Defoe (1928), I, 13–14.  5. Thrupp, 118.
6. Quoted in Fisher, 127.  7. Chambers, 106.

CHAPTER 2 (pp. 15–38).
1. Quoted in Tawney and Power, I, 74.
2. Quoted in Ashton (1955), 30.  3.Quoted in Stone (1965), 555.
4. Quoted in Cliffe, 114.  5. Quoted in Campbell, 224.
6. Smith, I, 363, 364.
7. Quoted in Tawney and Power, III, 71.
8. This is one of a series of such proclamations in the early seventeenth century. See Larkin and Hughes, nos 11, 23, 48, 143, 158, 166, 235, 236.
9. Quoted in Tawney and Power, I, 74–5.
10. Defoe (1928), I, 15.  11. *Ibid.*, II, 89.  12. Bacon, 101.
13. Quoted in Jones, 618.  14. Massie, 24.
15. Quoted in Glass and Eversley, 342.
16. Quoted in Tawney and Power, II, 189.
17. Quoted in Dyer, 167.  18. Quoted in Clark and Slack, 169.
19. Quoted in Appleby, 419–20.
20. Shakespeare, *A Midsummer Night's Dream*, Act II, Scene I.
21. Quoted in Tawney and Power, II, 341–2.
22. Quoted in Fisher, 122.  23. Quoted in Thirsk, 672.

24. Quoted in Laslett (1971), 121–2.
25. Quoted in Clark and Slack, 171.
26. Quoted in Creighton, II, 73.
27. Quoted in Ashton (1959), 19.
28. Drummond and Wilbraham, 81.
29. Quoted in Tawney and Power, III, 52.
30. Quoted in Drummond and Wilbraham, 192, 194.
31. Dekker, 108.


CHAPTER 3 (pp. 39–58).
1. Copeman, 133.   2. Quoted in Creighton, II, 308.
3. Dekker, 107.   4. Quoted in Copeman, 131.
5. Pepys, *Diary*, 18 July 1664, 23 January 1669.
6. Quoted in Creighton, I, 383–4.   7. *Ibid.*, II, 31.
8. *Ibid.*, I, 549.   9. *Ibid.*, II, 94.   10. *Ibid.*, II, 214.
11. Eaton, 40, 89, 134.   12. Quoted in Creighton, I, 262.
13. Quoted in Fisher, 125–6.
14. Evelyn, *Diary*, 15 October 1675.
15. Quoted in Creighton, II, 350.   16. *Ibid.*, II, 750.
17. Quoted in Waugh, 196.   18. *Ibid.*, 197.
19. Aubrey, 200, 414–15.   20. Quoted in Emmison (1973), 35.
21. Aubrey, 245.   22. *Ibid.*, 25.
23. Quoted in Creighton, II, 436.   24. Eaton, 99.
25. Aubrey, 250.   26. Browne, 149.   27. *Ibid.*, 157.


CHAPTER 4 (pp. 59–86).
1. Quoted in Morris, 207.   2. Quoted in Shrewsbury, 189.
3. *Calendar of State Papers, Domestic, 1547–80*, 235.
4. Quoted in Creighton, I, 306.   5. Quoted in Shrewsbury, 226.
6. This and the following quotations are taken from Dekker, 27–35.
7. Quoted in Creighton, I, 490–1.
8. This and the following quotations are taken from 'The Fearful Summer: or London's Calamitie . . .', in Taylor, *Works*.
9. Pepys, *Diary*, 22 November 1665.
10. The following quotations are taken from Defoe (1966), 110–18.
11. Pepys, *Diary*, 26 October, 30 November, 31 December 1665.
12. Aubrey, 25.   13. Helleiner, 85.

CHAPTER 5 (pp. 87–113).
1. Quoted in Dekker, 245.   2. *Ibid.*, 137.
3. Quoted in Copeman, 31–2.
4. Boorde, 'Prologue' (no pagination).   5. *Ibid.*
6. Quoted in Keynes, 67.   7. *Ibid.*, 70.   8. *Ibid.*, 15.
9. Quoted in Copeman, 120–1.
10. Taylor, 'The Fearful Summer . . .'   11. Aubrey, 27.
12. British Museum, Lansdowne MSS, 20, f. 10.
13. Quoted in Keynes, 439.   14. Aubrey, 27.   15. Dekker, 36.
16. *Ibid.*, 83, 86.   17. Aubrey, 379.   18. *Ibid.*, 289–90.
19. Dekker, 37.   20. Defoe (1966), 51, 53.
21. Quoted in Keynes, 217.   22. *Ibid.*, 218.
23. Quoted in Thomas, 316.   24. *Ibid.*, 177.
25. Quoted in Creighton, I, 674.   26. Quoted in Thomas, 181.
27. *Ibid.*, 187.   28. Aubrey, 27.   29. *Ibid.*, 92.
30. Cox (1898), 217.   31. Quoted in Reddaway, 208.
32. Cox (1898), 297–8.   33. Quoted in Reddaway, 287–8.
34. The *Orders* are printed in Defoe (1966), 57–66.
35. Quoted in Copeman, 156, 165, 170.


CHAPTER 6 (pp. 114–49).
1. Dekker, 25–6.   2. Elton (1972), 5.   3. Bacon, 59.
4. Clark (1958), 9–10.
5. Quoted in Firth, 145.   6. Dekker, 109.
7. Quoted in Firth, 255.   8. *Ibid.*, 223.
9. Quoted in Radzinowicz, 3.   10. *Ibid.*, 29.   11. *Ibid.*, 140.
12. *Ibid.*, 140–1.   13. *Ibid.*, 454, 468–9.   14. Aubrey, 23–4.
15. Quoted in Clark (1958), 37.   16. Larkin and Hughes, no. 160.
17. Quoted in Clark (1958), 38.
18. Larkin and Hughes, no. 126.   19. Aubrey, 24, 299.
20. Quoted in Emmison (1970), 149.
21. Quoted in Hutchins, 51.   22. *Ibid.*, 27.   23. *Ibid.*, 64, 68–9.
24. Quoted in Davis, 154.   25. Aubrey, 68.
26. All these incidents are taken from Cox (1974), 128, 131, 135.


CHAPTER 7 (pp. 150–74).
1. Browne, 123.   2. Quoted in Hole, 220–1.
3. Quoted in Stone (1973), 54–5.   4. Browne, 137.
5. Quoted in Cox (1974), 120, 121.

6. Misson, entry under 'Funerals'.

7. Quoted in Stone (1965), 579.    8. Larkin and Hughes, no. 229.

9. Quoted in Cox (1974), 121, 122.    10. *Ibid.*, 124.

11. Misson, 'Funerals'.    12. *Ibid.*    13. Quoted in Burley, 290.

14. Quoted in Keynes, 415.    15. Aubrey, 292.

16. Quoted in Macfarlane, *Josselin*, 100.    17. Misson, 'Funerals'.

18. Evelyn, *Diary*, 12 February 1682–/3.    19. Stow, 311–12, 391.

20. *Journals of the House of Commons*, Vol. 25, 274.

21. Quoted in Macfarlane, *Josselin*, 100.

22. Misson, 'Funerals'.    23. Quoted in Hole, 228.

24. Quoted in Macfarlane, *Josselin*, 100.

25. Quoted in Stone (1965), 577.

26. Quoted in Cox (1974), 117.    27. *Ibid.*, 114, 126.

28. Aubrey, 153.    29. Stone (1965), 579–80.

30. Quoted in Esdaile (1943), 362.    31. *Ibid.*, 365.

32. Quoted in Stone (1965), 577.    33. Quoted in Cliffe, 127.

34. Quoted in George, 303.    35. Quoted in Campbell, 387–8.

36. Quoted in Hole, 232.

37. Shakespeare, *The Winter's Tale*, Act III, Scene II.

38. Quoted in Macfarlane, *Josselin*, 166.    39. Aubrey, 23.

40. Evelyn, *Diary*, 27 January 1657/8.

# Bibliography

This is not a comprehensive bibliography of demographic history, but a list of books and articles I have found useful. References having a particular bearing on historical demography are marked with an asterisk (*).

*A. B. Appleby, 'Disease or Famine? Mortality in Cumberland and Westmorland, 1580–1640', *Econ. Hist. Rev.*, 2nd ser., Vol. XXVI (1973).

T. S. Ashton, *An Economic History of England: The Eighteenth Century*, London 1955.

T. S. Ashton, *Economic Fluctuations in England, 1700–1800*, Oxford 1959.

John Aubrey, *Aubrey's Brief Lives*, ed O. L. Dick, Penguin ed., Harmondsworth 1972.

Francis Bacon, *Essays*, World Classics ed., London 1937.

*J. M. W. Bean, 'Plague, Population and Economic Decline in the Later Middle Ages', *Econ. Hist. Rev.*, 2nd ser., Vol. XV (1963).

W. G. Bell, *The Great Plague in London in 1665*, London 1924.

A. Boorde, *The Breviary of Health* (1547), facsimile ed., Amsterdam and New York 1971.

*A. R. Bridbury, 'The Black Death', *Econ. Hist. Rev.*, 2nd ser. Vol. XXVI (1973).

Sir Thomas Browne, *Religio Medici and Other Writings*, ed C. H. Hertford, London 1906.

K. H. Burley, 'An Essex Clothier of the Eighteenth Century', *Econ. Hist. Rev.*, 2nd ser., Vol. XI (1958).

A. H. Burne and P. Young, *The Great Civil War*, London 1959.

M. Campbell, *The English Yeoman Under Elizabeth and the Early Stuarts*, New Haven 1942.

*J. D. Chambers, *Population, Economy, and Society in Pre-Industrial England*, London 1972.

K. Charlton, 'The Professions in Sixteenth-Century England', *University of Birmingham Hist. Jnl*, Vol. XII (1969).

G. N. Clark, *The Later Stuarts, 1660–1714,* 2nd ed., Oxford 1956.

G. N. Clark, *War and Society in the Seventeenth Century,* London 1958.

P. Clark and P. Slack, ed., *Crisis and Order in English Towns, 1500–1700,* London 1972.

J. T. Cliffe, *The Yorkshire Gentry from the Reformation to the Civil War,* London 1969.

W. S. C. Copeman, *Doctors and Diseases in Tudor Times,* London 1960.

*J. Cornwall, 'English Population in the Early Sixteenth Century', *Econ. Hist. Rev.,* 2nd ser., Vol. XXIII (1970).

J. C. Cox, *The Parish Registers of England,* 2nd ed., Wakefield 1974.

J. C. Cox, ed., *Records of the Borough of Northampton,* Vol. II, Northampton 1898.

*C. Creighton, *A History of Epidemics in England,* 2 vols, 2nd ed., London 1965.

C. Cruickshank, *Elizabeth's Army,* 2nd ed., Oxford 1966.

R. Davis, *The Rise of the English Shipping Industry in the Seventeenth and Eighteenth Centuries,* London 1962.

D. Defoe, *A Tour Through England and Wales* (1724–26), 2 vols, ed. G. D. H. Cole, London 1928.

D. Defoe, *A Journal of the Plague Year* (1722), Penguin ed., Harmondsworth 1966.

T. Dekker, *The Plague Pamphlets of Thomas Dekker,* ed. F. P. Wilson, Oxford 1925.

J. C. Drummond and A. Wilbraham, *The Englishman's Food,* revised ed., London 1957.

S. Dumas, *Losses of Life Caused by War,* Oxford 1923.

*A. D. Dyer, *The City of Worcester in the Sixteenth Century,* Leicester 1973.

D. Eaton, *The Letters of Daniel Eaton to the Third Earl of Cardigan, 1725–1732,* ed. J. Wake and D. C. Webster (Northants Records Soc., Vol. XXIV), Kettering 1971.

G. R. Elton, *England Under the Tudors,* London 1955.

G. R. Elton, *Policy and Police: The Enforcement of the Reformation in the Age of Thomas Cromwell,* London 1972.

F. G. Emmison, *Elizabethan Life: Disorder,* Chelmsford 1970.

F. G. Emmison, *Elizabethan Life: Morals and the Church Courts,* Chelmsford 1973.

K. Esdaile, 'Sculpture and Sculptors in Yorkshire', *Yorks. Archaeological Jnl,* Vols. XXV (1943) and XXVI (1944).

John Evelyn, *The Diary of John Evelyn*, Globe ed., ed. A. Dobson, London 1908.

M. E. Finch, *The Wealth of Five Northamptonshire Families, 1540–1640* (Northants Records Soc., Vol. XIX), Oxford 1956.

C. H. Firth, *Cromwell's Army*, 4th ed., London 1962.

*F. J. Fisher, 'Influenza and Inflation in Tudor England', *Econ. Hist. Rev.*, 2nd ser., Vol. XVIII (1965).

M. D. George, *London Life in the Eighteenth Century*, 2nd ed., London 1965.

*D. V. Glass and D. E. C. Eversley, ed., *Population in History: Essays in Historical Demography*, London 1965.

*A. Gooder, 'The Population Crisis of 1727–30 in Warwickshire' in *Midland History*, Vol. I, London 1972.

M. Greenwood, *Epidemics and Crowd Diseases*, London 1935.

*H. J. Habakkuk, *Population Growth and Economic Development since 1750*, Leicester 1971.

H. W. Haggard, *Devils, Drugs and Doctors*, London 1929.

K. F. Helleiner, 'The Population of Europe from the Black Death to the Eve of the Vital Revolution' in *The Cambridge Economic History of Europe*, Vol. IV, ed. E. E. Rich and C. H. Wilson, London 1967.

C. Hole, *The English Housewife in the Seventeenth Century*, London 1953.

*T. H. Hollingsworth, 'The Demography of the British Peerage', *Population Studies*, Vol. XVIII, Supplement (1965).

*T. H. Hollingsworth, *Historical Demography*, London 1969.

W. G. Hoskins, *Provincial England*, London 1963.

W. G. Hoskins, 'Harvest Fluctuations and English Economic History, 1480–1619', *Agricultural Hist. Rev.*, Vol. XII (1964).

W. G. Hoskins, 'Harvest Fluctuations and English Economic History, 1620–1759', *Agricultural Hist. Rev.*, Vol. XVI (1968).

*W. G. Howson, 'Plague, Poverty and Population in Parts of North-west England, 1580–1720', *Trans. Hist. Soc. of Lancs. and Cheshire*, Vol. CXXII (1961).

J. H. Hutchins, *Jonas Hanway, 1712–1786*, London 1940.

E. L. Jones, 'The Condition of English Agriculture, 1500–1640', *Econ. Hist. Rev.*, 2nd ser., Vol. XXI (1968).

E. Kerridge, *The Agricultural Revolution*, London 1967.

Sir G. Keynes, *The Life of William Harvey*, Oxford 1966.

J. F. Larkin and P. L. Hughes, ed., *Stuart Royal Proclamations*, Vol. I, Oxford 1973.

*P. Laslett, 'Size and Structure of the Household in England over Three Centuries', *Population Studies*, Vol. XXII (1969).

*P. Laslett, *The World We Have Lost*, 2nd ed., London 1971.

A. Macfarlane, *The Family Life of Ralph Josselin*, London 1970.

A. Macfarlane, *Witchcraft in Tudor and Stuart England*, London 1970.

R. Margotta, *An Illustrated History of Medicine*, London 1968.

J. Massie, *Considerations on the Leather Trade of Great Britain*, London 1757.

H. Misson, *Memoirs and Observations in his Travels over England . . .*, London 1719.

C. Morris, 'The Plague in Britain', *The Historical Jnl*, Vol. XIV (1971).

D. Ogg, *England in the Reigns of James II and William III*, Oxford 1955.

Samuel Pepys, *The Diary of Samuel Pepys*, transcribed and ed. by R. Latham and W. Matthews, London 1971.

*E. H. Phelps Brown and S. V. Hopkins, 'Wages Rates and Prices : Evidence for Population Pressure in the Sixteenth Century', *Economica*, new ser., Vol. XXIV (1957).

J. Pound, *Poverty and Vagrancy in Tudor England*, London 1971.

B. Puckle, *Funeral Customs: Their Origin and Development*, London 1926.

L. Radzinowicz, *A History of the English Criminal Law and its Administration from 1750*, Vol. I, London 1948.

*P. Razzell, 'Population Change in Eighteenth Century England : A Re-interpretation', *Econ. Hist. Rev.*, 2nd ser., Vol. XVIII (1967).

T. F. Reddaway, *The Rebuilding of London after the Great Fire*, London 1940.

M. Roberts, *The Military Revolution, 1560–1660*, Belfast 1956.

R. S. Roberts, 'The Personnel and Practice of Medicine in Tudor and Stuart England', Pt I, *Medical History*, Vol. VI (1962); Pt II, *Medical History*, Vol. VIII (1964).

R. S. Roberts, 'A Consideration of the Nature of the English Sweating Sickness', *Medical History*, Vol. IX (1965).

G. Rudé, *Hanoverian London, 1714–1808*, London 1971.

*J. Saltmarsh, 'Plague and Economic Decline in England in the Later Middle Ages', *Cambridge Hist. Jnl*, Vol. VII (1941).

J. F. D. Shrewsbury, *A History of Bubonic Plague in the British Isles*, London 1970.

C. J. Singer and E. A. Underwood, *A Short History of Medicine*, 2nd ed., Oxford 1962.

Adam Smith, *An Inquiry into the Nature and Causes of the Wealth of Nations* (1776), Everyman ed., 2 vols, London 1910.

L. Stone, *The Crisis of the Aristocracy, 1540–1642*, Oxford 1965.

L. Stone, *Family and Fortune*, Oxford 1973.

J. Stow, *A Survey of London* (1598), ed. H. Morley, London, n.d.

*I. Sutherland, 'When Was the Great Plague? Mortality in London, 1563 to 1665' in D. V. Glass and R. Revelle, ed., *Population and Social Change*, London 1972.

R. D. Tawney and E. Power, *Tudor Economic Documents*, 3 vols, London 1924.

John Taylor, *The Fearful Summer: or London's Calamitie* . . . (1625) in *The Works of John Taylor the Water Poet*, Spencer Society ed., London 1873.

J. Thirsk, ed., *The Agrarian History of England and Wales*, Vol. IV : *1500–1640*, London 1967.

K. Thomas, *Religion and the Decline of Magic*, London 1971.

*S. Thrupp, 'The Problem of Replacement Rates in Late Medieval Population', *Econ. Hist. Rev.*, 2nd ser., Vol. XVIII (1965).

M. A. Waugh, 'Venereal Diseases in Sixteenth-Century England', *Medical History*, Vol. XVII (1973).

J. A. Williamson, *The Tudor Age*, 3rd ed., London 1964.

*E. A. Wrigley, 'Family Limitation in Pre-Industrial England', *Econ. Hist. Rev.*, 2nd ser., Vol. XIX (1966).

*E. A. Wrigley, ed., *An Introduction to English Historical Demography*, London 1966.

*E. A. Wrigley, *Population and History*, London 1969.

*E. A. Wrigley, 'Mortality in Pre-Industrial England : the Example of Colyton, Devon, over Three Centuries' in D. V. Glass and R. Revelle, ed., *Population and Social Change*, London 1972.

P. Ziegler, *The Black Death*, London 1969.

H. Zinsser, *Rats, Lice, and History*, London 1935.

# Index